making
sexuality
human

W. NORMAN PITTENGER

•

PILGRIM PRESS
PHILADELPHIA

Second printing 1972
Third printing 1975

SBN 8298–0183–9
LIBRARY OF CONGRESS CATALOG CARD NUMBER 79–126862

COPYRIGHT © 1970 UNITED CHURCH PRESS
PHILADELPHIA, PENNSYLVANIA

contents

Chapter 1
The Problem of Sexuality Today

A few days before beginning this book I read in a weekly journal the report of a "sounding," taken by one of the mass-opinion agencies, of the views of a cross-section of the public on matters of sexual morality. Opinion was by no means unanimous, but on questions such as the permissibility of sexual relations of young people before marriage, the acceptability of literary, dramatic, and cinematographic discussion of sex and portrayal of sexual contacts, the right of homosexuals to engage in physical acts without incurring condemnation for "unnatural" behaviour, the availability of divorce for those who found their marriages intolerable, and similar issues, the large majority of those questioned took what nowadays is styled a highly "permissive" attitude. It was interesting to note that they said that they did not think that the whole moral structure of western society was collapsing; they did think, however, that we were entering upon an age when more honest and open avowal of sexual interests and more liberal attitudes towards sexual matters generally were replacing a less honest, less open, and less liberal point-of-view. And the great majority of respondents said that in their opinion this was a better situation than the earlier one, since it made it necessary for those who presented sexual moral standards to offer a convincing and reasonable case for such standards, rather than to rely on inherited conventional ideas or legal means of enforcement.

Now it so happened that a week or two earlier I had read in a daily newspaper the address of a prominent ecclesiastical dignitary who had discussed the same subject. His address was largely a long series of laments about relaxed attitudes on sexual morality, shocking violations of the common decencies, easy acceptance of homosexuality as well as of general sexual promiscuity, indecent plays and films and pornographic novels —all of which, he said, were an outrageous violation of Christian ethical principles. He urged legal action to prevent some of these, and moral condemnation as a way of meeting others. At no point did this spokesman for Christian morality, as he regarded himself, speak understandingly of what is going on in the sphere of sexual relationships, nor did he show any readiness to make a case for the position which he assumed to be the right—and the Christian—one.

These two journalistic reports made one person, at least, realize how wide a gulf there is between popular feeling, on the one hand, and at least *some* Christian thought, on the other. I write "some" because I am by no means unaware of the efforts being made in Britain, in North America, and in many circles on the continent of Europe—perhaps elsewhere as well—to work through to a genuinely Christian and honestly argued statement of Christian views on sexuality. But I should also say that on the whole our greatest need is for a *theological* appraisal of sexuality, in the light of the main emphases in Christian faith and with due regard for contemporary attitudes and behaviour-patterns. Before any moral pattern is advanced, whether that should be the traditional one or a radically altered one, we require a careful consideration of sexuality from the point of view of Christian faith as it works itself out theologically.

If Christian faith, from whatever angle we approach it and with whatever phrasing we feel sound, is in fact an opening of truth, *if* God and man and the world are best understood in the light of those events in history from which Christianity takes its rise and of that response to such events which constitutes the essence of Christian commitment, what can we, what must we, say about human sexuality? That man is a sexual being is apparent; that he has sexual drive, urgent desire for sexual contacts, and the deep feeling that one of the central areas of human fulfilment is sexual, we cannot for a moment deny. What does all this *mean,* from the stance of Christian faith?

During the history of Christian theology much has been said about this

8

sexual aspect of human experience. But all too frequently there has been no attempt to develop a specifically Christian—which might perhaps also be a specifically human—interpretation of the obvious fact of human sexuality. Sometimes, indeed, the attitude has been one of regret for man's sexual drive—it is accepted as a fact but regarded as a rather unhappy and unfortunate fact. Yet at the same time the exaltation of marriage as an "estate" blessed of God and good for men has indicated that sexuality is not altogether condemned. At least within the limits of marriage, sex is a good thing—at the *very* least, a permissible thing. On the whole, however, a very considerable portion of Christian history has been unwilling to say much more than that, while the tendency in many circles to exalt "virginity" or "celibacy" as a higher state than marriage has given the impression that the acceptance of sex, even in marriage, is little more than a grudging consent to an inescapable fact, rather than a glad recognition of one of the truly good things in God's creation.

In a number of books and in several essays, I myself have had something to say about sexuality. Most of this has been incidental to a discussion of some other theme. For example, in writing about "the Christian understanding of human nature," it was inevitable that one chapter should have taken into account the sexuality of man. In pleading for a more generous attitude to male and female homosexuals, in a small paperback, I naturally devoted one short section to a consideration of sexual drives. And in a series of publications on the significance of love, both human and divine, as a clue to the meaning of Christian faith and the best understanding of the human situation, some treatment of sexuality was inevitably included. What I propose to do in the present study, however, is to give full attention to this subject. In other words, as its title shows, this book is intended as a small contribution to the necessary task of working out a Christian theology of sex.

Obviously much will remain to be done. I do not think, for a moment, that what I shall be saying will be an exhaustive treatment, much less a conclusive or final one. A great deal of work remains to be done, by a great many different religious traditions, and with a great deal more knowledge than I am able to claim. Yet it may be that a book like this one, with all its defects and omissions, may be useful in awakening others to the need for just such a full-scale and full-length study as I believe is required. Many years ago, I was asked to write a series of articles for an American religious journal which sought to get "answers" to the celebrated Kinsey Reports on Human Sexuality. Those articles, later incorporated in a small volume entitled *The Christian View of Sexual Be-*

haviour, represented a view which I now feel to have been altogether too conventional. They were my first, and not very well considered, response to a new situation in respect to sexual life—a situation which is reflected, much more openly and honestly, in the report of the "soundings" to which I referred at the beginning of this chapter. My present effort, then, is in some ways a reversal, even a denial, of some things said in that series of articles. But that is because I have come to see, for a variety of reasons, that I had not really been aware of all that is involved in sexuality, nor had I grasped as I do now the utter centrality of the sexual drive in human personality and in human social relationships.

That centrality will be emphasized in the sequel. We owe our increasing realization of this very largely to the work of Sigmund Freud. Whatever may have been exaggerated or erroneous in his teaching, this at least was his correct evaluation of human existence—man's sexual drive, his *libido,* is at the very heart of that existence. To fail to see this is to be blind to the truth about oneself and about every man or woman known to us. Nor does this mean that we are obsessed by sexual matters.

A very distinguished churchman once said in my hearing that he was convinced that "younger people," as he called them, were indeed thus "obsessed." Unfortunately he went on to remark that in his view sex was simply enough described: it was the human desire to possess and control other people. Knowing him to be happily married, with a large and devoted family, I was astounded at his remark. But I recognized at the time, and I emphasize now, that the *distrust* of sex, the *dislike* of it, the *distaste* at any discussion of it, such as this churchman showed, are very typical of a good deal of conventional religious thinking. Very few people, thank heaven, would identify sexuality with human pride and self-assertion, as he did; but a great many would wish to say nothing about the subject or, when they were forced to speak, would do so in a disdainful and even condemnatory manner. What a tragedy that is! And how plainly it reflects the gulf between ordinary human experience, as modern people know it, and the general ecclesiastical line of thought.

Furthermore, his comments revealed all too clearly a prevalent tendency on the part of many churchmen to take a negative attitude towards sexual matters. If "younger people," in his own words, including a number of younger clergymen, seem to be "obsessed" by the question of sex, this is in violent reaction from the much more frequent policy of saying nothing about the subject save in terms of alarm, fear, or denial. The pendulum swings to the opposite extreme. What is required of us is neither an "obsession" about sex nor a negation of sex, but a forthright posi-

10

tive attitude towards it. For myself, I think that the so much criticized "younger people," within and without the religious community, are healthily accepting the facts and that what *appears* to be "obsession" is simply this readiness to accept and to talk positively and constructively about the matter.

Nor is the appearance on the stage of a number of plays which deal with the subject, not to speak of books and films, a sign of moral corruption. It could only seem so to those who would prefer to hide the matter in a dark corner. But precisely because human sexuality is so central, it refuses to be hidden. When it is not accepted positively, it reappears in an ugly guise. The negative attitude is all too likely to become a *warped* attitude; then we have the horrible spectacle of a kind of "inverted virginity," to use a phrase of Mr. W. H. Auden's with its appalling consequences in a twisting and distorting of personality. The phenomenon of "spinsterhood," much more common among men than among women, manifests itself. This "spinsterhood" is not simply the state of being unmarried or of making no overt expression of sexual desires—that would not be harmful, since there have been many men and women who either by vocation (monks or nuns) or by choice (decision to remain unmarried, in order to devote one's entire effort to some cause which makes enormous demands) or by necessity (inability to find a husband or wife or sexual partner with whom one may have a long-term relationship) are in no position to express overtly their sexual instinct. No. What is seen often enough is a kind of killing of human sexuality, in which this aspect of man's vitality is trampled on, suppressed, denied with horror. The result of that sort of thing is a quite terrible perversion of human personality. Perhaps all of us have met people like this; they are thoroughly unattractive, but what is worse is that they are often thoroughly inhuman in their attitudes and actions. Most of us would prefer a person who without any restraint expresses his sexuality, for he at least is human—some would think *too* human—and his excesses are the over-manifestation of a drive that in itself is good, not the murdering of a drive that he has taken to be bad.

Like everything else in human experience, like every other area of human activity and behaviour, man's sexual life needs to be controlled. But that is very different from saying that it should be denied, repressed, or regarded in a negative way. It is precisely because sexuality is *good* that it should not be "used" without any respect for norms, whatever they may be, which will promote and provide for the best possible expression of such a good thing. The point of control is simply that, despite the popular saying, one *can* have "too much of a good thing." Too much, here, merely indicates that there is always the possibility of a jaded, tired outlook on sex, and a lack of restraint which will, so to say, "take the gilding off" and leave a bad taste in the mouth. This, as I shall hope to show, is the reason for the control of human sexuality; and it is a good and sound reason. The kind of control which is really negation is a bad kind of control; indeed, it is not control at all, but outright rejection of a wonderful and beautiful "gift of God" to his human children.

During the week in which this chapter is being written, a well-known journalist wrote in *The Spectator* (7 June 1969) an article in which he expressed his views of the Christian church and the Christian faith. In the course of this article, Mr. Ludovic Kennedy said that the church exists "to give comfort to the lonely, the guilty, and the afraid"—and that since fewer people today are lonely, almost none have a sense of guilt, and fear (even of death) is diminishing and will continue to do so, there is nothing left for the church to do. It is tragic that Mr. Kennedy, during what he calls "ten years hard at prep and public school, chapel once a day and twice on Sundays, Scripture or Divinity classes from six to seventeen, and Confirmation too," never once learned what the Christian church is really here for, nor what the Christian faith is about. The fault may very well be in those who were supposed to teach him; but whoever is at fault, the fact of his failure is clear.

The relevance of this for our present concern should be obvious. What has Christianity to say about sexuality? What conceivable contribution can it make to our thinking about this matter? Mr. Kennedy says that "young people prefer to base their behaviour on mutual respect and consideration rather than because of what some self-created God"—whatever that means!—"or gods may have determined for them." He adds that he does "not think that their failure rate is any greater than that of their Christian predecessors." Now I should wish to say that here the inadequacy of Mr. Kennedy's teachers or his own lack of understanding of what *perhaps* they taught is most clearly shown. For it is precisely in "mutual respect and consideration" that we express what God has "determined" should be done. And this provides us with a clue which we may follow a considerable way.

For the Christian faith is no matter of good behaviour, nor is it an interesting speculation about God, "self-created" or otherwise. The Christian faith is the commitment of self to the reality of the cosmic Love which is in and behind and through and under all creaturely experience. In consequence of that commitment, which the Christian believes himself

12

enabled to make because he has been grasped by such Love in the Man of Nazareth, the Christian ought to have a perspective on life which enables him to see very deeply into the significance of the world and of himself in the world. The Christian church exists to further that commitment as it proclaims the activity of cosmic Love in the Jesus about whom it teaches and preaches. It exists to enable men and women to relate themselves, in a social way, to that Love—consciously, intentionally, and attentively—and thus to find "wholeness of life." If it is not doing these things, but instead is busying itself with intra-group affairs, it is a failure; it is disobedient to its Lord and his purpose for it.

But once this is understood, then the perspective on life which Christian commitment in faith makes possible will have consequences that are very far-reaching. Every area of human experience will be affected—not least the area of sexual desire and drive, so central in that experience. This does not suggest that Christian men and women will have a different *kind* of sexuality than do others; but it does mean that they will understand their sexuality in a distinctive way. Maybe that distinctive way is the really *human* way, although if we say this (as I think we should) we must not suppose that nobody save a Christian can see things thus. To suppose that would imply that God does not disclose his purpose to any save Christians, which is both blasphemous and absurd. Wherever men have come to some deep understanding, some illuminating awareness, of the meaning of their sexuality—as of other aspects of their experience—they are recipients of an insight which ultimately is God-given although humanly conveyed and appreciated. The thing a Christian wishes to claim is that these point towards a perspective which is true; a perspective which is validated through the Christian faith itself.

Any such position, however, will be impossible to maintain if we succumb to that negative attitude which has dogged so much traditional thinking about human sexuality. Yet the negative attitude is *not* tied in with, nor is it an integral part, of the Christian perspective. On the contrary, however distinguished may have been those who took such a denying position, whether in the past or at the present moment, it is nothing but a contradiction of the positive view which is implied, nay demanded, if the Christian stance be true at all. This is why so many of us today are convinced that this matter of sexuality is of first importance. It is not that we are "obsessed" by sexuality, but that we agree with Freud—and before him, unlikely as it may seem, with St. Augustine—that human sexual instincts, drives, and desires are utterly central and enormously important as indicative of what man *is,* what God purposes for man, and what is the highest and best human possibility. Alas, St. Augustine took what was a sound view and distorted it to make sexuality principally the occasion for human sin and guilt. But this need not have been the case; and one of our urgent necessities today is to show that it is *not* the case.

Certainly, because of its centrality, sexuality *may become* an occasion for the distortion of human personality. On the other hand, and much more significantly, it may become the occasion for the fulfilment of human potentiality in such a way that our existence is glorified and our whole movement towards "becoming human" given both dignity and beauty. My friend Canon Louis Weil of the Episcopal Theological Seminary of the Caribbean has said, in an essay on liturgy, that Christians should always be prepared to "affirm the world to be good" for "it is God's world and . . . he has created man in it to live abundantly." And Dr. Paul Lehmann, writing in *Ethics in a Christian Context,* insists that so far as human existence is concerned God's purpose is "making and keeping human life human." These two comments belong together. The world, as God's creation, is a *good* world and in it men are to find opportunity for "abundant life"; life of that sort *is* human life—and we should see to it that it is kept so.

Human life—and sexuality is central to that life. Hence it too is good; it too is to be an aid to abundance of living; and it also must be kept human. That is the way in which it can be understood, from the Christian perspective. And since the affirmation of Christian faith, as I have urged in my remarks about Mr. Ludovic Kennedy's misunderstandings, is that in and through, beyond and behind, below and above this human life is the cosmic Love, the cosmic Lover if you will, while (as I shall argue in the next chapter) man himself is a creaturely lover-in-the-making, we must come to realize that human sexuality is part of that pattern of love, both human and divine. This realization will prevent us from trivializing human sexuality; at the same time it will enable us to avoid turning it into that parody of love, so often found amongst the moralists: a matter of legal enactment, hemmed in by the sort of rule-making and rule-keeping which destroys spontaneity and freedom. Yet I repeat again that control of some type is necessary here, as elsewhere; the question is *what* type of control and the protest I am making is against the legalism of certain ethical systems, not against the requirement that every good thing must be used with a restraint that is indeed characteristic of any properly human good.

But "restraint" is not a fortunate word here, although I cannot find a better one. For restraint can mean denial of spontaneity and freedom, an

14

equally negative attitude; and what I am talking about is nothing like that. My intention is only to say that when we have grasped the theological meaning of human sexuality we shall come to see that sexual expression includes in itself or entails principles which will serve and which do serve towards the best, richest, and most rewarding exercise of our sexual capacities. Above all, we shall be aware of the need for a *direction* in sexual expression which will be intimately related to the "becoming," the making real or actual, of man's potentialities.

This brings us to the final point in this introductory chapter. I have spoken of Christian faith and its meaning; now I wish to argue that this faith does not stand without any context. Any deeply-held conviction, any human commitment, is always "in context." It is my strong belief that the most satisfactory context available to us today is the conceptuality which in North America and elsewhere goes by the name of "process thought." This is not the place to outline in detail the various elements in this conceptuality; I have sought to do this elsewhere, notably in my book *Process Thought and Christian Faith* (London: Nisbet; New York: Macmillan, 1968). All I need say here is that I am speaking of a general world-view which sees the entire cosmos, including man, and that divine reality whom we call God, in a dynamic, vital, processive, and societal (or organic) fashion. Things are on the move, as evolutionary science has taught us; nothing and nobody remains fixed in one definite spot. God himself, while eternal in his steadfastness and faithfulness, is concretely in movement, making things new and sharing in their novelty. The world as a whole is a changing pattern, even if the change seems sometimes to be very slow while at other times it appears very rapid. And man is "on the go," too. What occurs in the world is a "happening," as people say these days; and man is a "happening," too.

In such a context, Christian faith sees no meaningless and irrelevant sequence of "one damned thing after another," but the working out of a purpose of Love. Human existence is part of that movement. Here is nothing mechanical or pre-determined, however; there is a radical freedom running through the cosmos, less obvious at certain levels but none the less real in its limited way. In man, both sound Christian thinking and intelligent observation insist, the freedom is much more conscious; we are aware of it and we feel a definite responsibility for the choices which we make. Thus there is no contradiction, in this conceptuality as a context for Christian faith and commitment, between God's purpose for men and their own decision, taken with the freedom that is appropriate to them, to move in this or that direction towards the fulfilment of their

15

potentialities in community with other men—and in relationship to the natural order as well as to the divine Love.

This has a profoundly important bearing on the way in which we think about human sexuality. At the level of human life sex is not merely animal—although it has animal elements in it; it is distinctively *human,* like everything else about man. The emergence of man in the cosmic order of development is the emergence of something which is genuinely new. The patterning of events which constitutes man as man is distinctive and different from other patternings. This means that all the "ingredients," as we might say, which are found in man are to be integrated into his ongoing purpose of becoming that which potentially he is: *man is to become man*—he is not that yet, in any given instance, but he is *on the way* to that goal. He is not solitary in this; he is in sociality with his fellowmen, for we are all knit together, bound up with each other, in the human enterprise. Our sexuality, so central to each of us, is meant to be integrated into the pattern of our moving towards societal fulfilment. It has a purposive quality, although most of the time this is not (and ought not to be) vividly and self-consciously in our minds.

A number of years ago, a popular musical comedy included a song whose refrain referred over and over again to "doing what comes naturally." We shall need to enquire into the proper sense of that adverb, "naturally," which can be given meanings that are not appropriate here. But when "naturally" is taken to signify "that which is in accord with the best direction for the fulfilment of human potentiality," we may rightly say that human sexuality ought to be a matter of "doing what comes naturally." As it is natural for man to be sexual and as man's very "nature" is to move towards making actual the possibilities (physical and spiritual, this-worldly and also in relation to his true end or goal) which are his, so in his sexual existence he is truest to himself and therefore truest to the divine intention for him as and when his sexual desire and drive is given the opportunity to express itself—and express itself in terms of love-in-action. In brief, *that* is the Christian theological understanding of the matter; or so I am convinced. The remainder of this book will be an attempt to amplify that brief statement.

Chapter 2
Human Personality in the Making

Man's sexuality is central to his nature; it is an essential and in many ways determinative aspect of his personality. But before we discuss that subject, we must know something about the setting of this sexuality in man as such. Hence we now turn to a consideration of human personality —human nature, as it used to be called—in order to provide a context for the following chapter, in which our full attention will be given to the sexual drive and its expression.

What *is* man? That has been a question which people have asked themselves for as long as they have been able to think reflectively about the world and about themselves living in that world. The answers they have given have been most various, ranging all the way from the view that after all man is only "another animal" to that which sees him, in the classical definition which St. Thomas Aquinas took over from Boethius, as "an individual substance of a rational nature." I do not intend to go over the field, so to say; in the book already mentioned, *The Christian Understanding of Human Nature,* I attempted a general survey and suggested my own statement of what man is and how he may be described. Instead

17

of repeating such a general survey, I shall here suggest what seem to me the essential factors in any adequate understanding of man's personality.

The first of these is implied in the word which has just been used: "personality." I believe that one of the serious difficulties with much that has been written about man in the traditional or conventional books is the failure to reckon with this fact of human personality. On the face of it, it is clear that to be "personal" is very different from being a "thing." Sticks and stones are things; perhaps one can call a tiger, a dog, or a cat a "thing"—although one hesitates a bit before doing so. But to think of a man as a "thing" is an outrage to human beings and is almost certain to lead us to a static conception of what it signifies to be human.

I take it that when we use the nouns "personality" or "person," or the adjective "personal," we include a number of notions that have great importance. Let me list some of them: awareness and self-awareness; capacity to communicate with others in the same category or class; ability to make decisions, with some sense of freedom and with due responsibility for the choices made. Along with these, we should also include some degree of integration, finding its focus in an aim or goal or purpose—however vaguely or dimly this may be apprehended. Furthermore, personality is characterized by the making of judgements, both moral and aesthetic; a person evaluates *this* as better or worse than *that,* and he appreciates *this* as more or less harmonious and appealing than *that.* In making such judgements, he feels drawn to or attracted by a given course of action, just as he appreciates a particular component in his environment as being "lovely" or compelling of admiration. These judgements are not infallible, of course; as I have said, it is "more" or "less"—but despite their relativity, they seem to human beings to have some validity and they are felt to be in some sort of correspondence with how things really "go" in the world apart from the subjective human awareness or the selectivity of the one who makes the judgement.

Thus I wish to start by observing that human beings are in fact "aware" of the world and they also know themselves *as being aware* of it. This means that they have *self*-consciousness. Child psychologists tell us that a sense of selfhood develops as very young children, hardly born, begin to see and know that there is something-not-themselves; in learning this, they come to recognize their own self-knowledge. They begin to think, rather than simply to react to what is outside them. Deeper than any surface experiences, deeper even than acceptance of mother and father and siblings and the material realities surrounding them, there is a gradual increase in an *ego*-centricity. Indeed for a time, it would seem, this awareness of the *ego,* as distinguished from other presumed *egos* and from environmental pressures, can become absolutely central to the young child. Yet, given enough experience, his ego-centricity is (so to say) "tamed"; and he comes to understand that others are like him, with their own selfhood. He must accommodate himself to them, he must "get along" with them, he must establish some sort of relationship with them which signifies that he is "in community" with those others. Nonetheless, he cannot escape, nor should he, from the awareness of himself in a vividly conscious fashion.

Precisely because there are those "others," however, he develops the capacity to communicate with them in meaningful ways. He learns words and this imitative process brings him to learn language—the method by which such communication is made possible at the level of significant interchange of ideas. At the same time, there is another kind of communication, in which words are not used but sharing is experienced through some mysterious participation in another's *presence.* There are feeling-tones here; there is a sense of being "one with" the other person, so that speech is not always necessary. It may be that this is the most profound type of communication possible for men—one thinks of Carlyle and Emerson sitting together for a whole evening, without uttering a single word, yet feeling that they were in genuine relationship and sharing in each other's lives. And certainly in the experience of deep affection, as between husband and wife or between intimate friends, speech is not necessary to establish and maintain a genuine participation of one with the other.

As to the ability to make decisions, little need be said. We all know that far down in our self-awareness as human personalities is this decision-making, this capacity to choose. The area in which our freedom to decide operates may not be so wide as libertarian thinkers have claimed; it is limited by the place and time where we live, by many circumambient factors over which we have no control, by our own past history and that of our family or class or group—and by much else. But granted these factors, no man can think of himself as completely *un*-free to decide, even if that decision is only to accept for himself the circumstances and conditions in which he finds himself or to refuse altogether to accept them in a rebellion which may very well be helpless and hopeless but most surely is *his own* rejection. Among the many possibilities which normally open before us, we do select this one rather than that

19

one. And we do it with some feeling of responsibility for the decision made. Even the most "helpless" of men would not deny a degree of that responsibility, despite his desire to escape from its consequences and to blame other people or the conditions in which he has lived (or some other agency) for what he has determined to do, to think, and to become.

We have spoken of personality, but it should be stressed that man is not a *finished* product but "personality in the making." Indeed that is what the term really means in our common experience. Someone once remarked to me, "A man who is not still growing, even when he reaches seventy or so, is to all intents and purposes dead." This I believe to be a true insight—for growth, in the sense of "becoming what one has it in one to be," is *the* mark of human personal existence. I should even venture to suggest—and doubtless be regarded as "heretical" for saying it— that God himself is to be regarded as, in at least one sense, "growing" or "developing"; by which I do not mean that he is becoming "more divine" or anything so nonsensical as that, but rather that in his relationships to the creation his divinity is enriched by that which he accepts, receives, and is affected by. He is no static entity but a living, active, dynamic reality who may be and ought to be conceived after the analogy of the best knowledge we ourselves possess of "personality." That is, he is best thought of in terms of the model of an open, receptive, self-giving man, who at the same time is *himself* in all his integrity. Obviously God is *more* than that; we ascribe such personality to him in an "eminent sense," as the Thomist philosophers would put it. But he is *at least* of that sort; and thus he must possess the capacity for such enrichment and expansion in relation to creation and in his own enjoyment of selfhood as we know in ourselves and in our fellowmen. But this is not the place to continue this discussion. My only intention in referring to it is to assert that if, as Christian faith declares, man is "made in the image of God," this illuminates for us not only our own manhood but also the character of God whose image we bear.

Man's *capacity* . . . yes; and that capacity is not yet completely realized. This suggests to us that as a personality in the making man is moving towards a goal. He is an "unfulfilled capacity"; and the direction of his human drive is towards fulfilment. That is to say, man is on the way to becoming human, rather than an instance of accomplished humanity.

One of the indelible aspects of our human existence is our awareness of this thrust towards the future. Whitehead and others have called this, in respect to man and to all other actual entities or occasions, their "subjective aim"—the phrase is a good one, since it includes both the reference to purpose or goal or end or objective *and* the subjectivity or selfhood which is involved in that thrust. At other levels of creation, this thrust is usually not vividly felt; there is no conscious awareness of what is going on. But with man, the thrust *is* both felt and known, in varying degrees of acuteness and specificity. One might almost call it, as David A. Pailin has done in an article which I cannot trace, a way of speaking of the human "vocation," the call to selfhood in relation to a purpose that lures man on and gives him an impetus or empowering which makes it impossible for him to rest entirely content "in one stay."

In an ultimate sense, fulfilment is possible only in God. But such a statement must be guarded from misunderstanding. Often enough, alas, we assume that "God" is always known as being exactly himself and divine, in this relationship with man. It has even been suggested, by a rather stupid popular writer on religious themes, that unless we *do* thus accurately identify God *as* God, we cannot know him at all. I believe that such an assertion is a denial of the patent fact that God is indeed omnipresent and that he works through and is revealed in the most various incognitos. The truth is that God is operative in whatever of good, truth, justice, beauty, love, concern, self-giving, and the like makes its impact on human existence and lures men to their proper fulfilment. All these are his *surrogates,* in the meaning of that word which my dictionary gives as primary; that is, they are his instruments or agents, acting for him and representing him. If they are taken as *substitutes* for God—by which I mean, if they are isolated from their context and made the *only* and the entirely humanly limited goals or ends or lures—they can become demonic, working against God and his purposes for men. But when they are seen in all their appeal as aiding in human fulfilment and are not narrowed to the merely "natural" (in the pejorative sense of the word), they are divine agents and agencies.

Thus the man who finds it difficult or impossible to say, "I believe in *God,*" may very well believe in him under one of those incognitos. He may adore and serve justice, for example; he may give himself, and hence find himself, in obedience to truth. This is why it is possible to say that no man can really be an atheist, even if he thinks himself to be one. The very fact of his finding *any* significance in his life is a manifestation of his having been found by what we Christians mean, or ought to mean, when we say "God." Nor does this entail God's being only a function of human experience, although some might interpret it thus. On the contrary, this is really a way in which the "more" in creation, the transcendent inexhaustibility working patiently and ceaselessly for the realization of that creation's genuine potentialities, is disclosed to men in their given situation. The Christian should not think that he is introducing men to a God whom otherwise and hitherto they have never encountered; what he *is* doing is giving a specific name to that which is inescapable for men. He is affirming that the personalized and personalizing Love which is seen in Jesus Christ and those who share his Spirit is the proper name of the reality which gives life significance and lures men towards their fulfilment or realization of the possibilities they possess—or that possess them.

As a personality in the making, man is not alone. He is *with others*. As we have noted, he possesses the capacity to communicate with others, either by words or in deeper "felt" participation; and this is a sign of his true *belonging*. To be on the way to becoming personal *is* to be ever more profoundly one with one's fellows, for personality is not the same as individuality. The latter signifies a given and particular isolable instance of a class; but personality means open-ness and receptivity and self-giving. Hence personality and sociality—man and society—are not separable. The man who is utterly self-contained and self-sufficient is indeed an individual, but it would be improper to think of him as truly a personal being, truly one on the way to realizing genuine personality.

The familiar words of John Donne come to mind: "No man is an island entire unto himself." As Donne goes on to say, continuing the use of his graphic image, every man is part of the "continent." Hence, when "the bell tolls" to announce a death, he urges, we need not ask "for whom it tolls," since "it tolls for *me*." Nor does this profound truth about human personality suggest only that "the more we are together, the happier we'll be," as someone has said. The kind of community or sociality which is in view does not necessarily involve continual physical presence with others, although that is by no means to be despised. What it does involve is the awareness of, participation in, and growing open-ness to, others of our race. We belong together, we are together, we develop together— that is the way things are in this world of ours. "It is not good for man to be alone," says the Genesis story; "God has set the solitary in families," says a prayer in one of the Anglican service books. All this is deeply and seriously *human*.

The reference in that prayer to "families" at once calls to mind the fact that for most human beings their sense of sociality finds its focus in the married state, with husband and wife and children. More will be said about this, in its relation to sexuality, in a later chapter. At this point, however, it is important to realize that while for *most* men and women, such familial relationships are their way towards self-realization in association with other humans, there are *some* for whom the most intimate spiritual and physical relationship must be with one of their own sex. These are the homosexuals, so much despised and so much attacked in Western culture—although today there is more sympathy for and understanding of their situation. We shall have something to say about them, too, in a later chapter. But it is also to be noted that although the focus of human social relationship is in the family, with another human being of differing sex, or in some sort of union with one of the same sex—as it were, a one-to-one relationship with the procreation of children to add to that relationship, so far as heterosexuals are concerned—there are other social contacts and modes of participation. There is the neighborhood, the town or village, the various associations which bring people together (societies, clubs, trades-unions, etc., etc.); and there is the race or nation or grouping in regions. Above all, there is the totality of manhood, including not only one's contemporaries but the long history of the human race out of which each of us emerged and to which we belong, as well as the future generations yet unborn to which also we belong. To contemplate *humanitas* in this wider aspect is to be brought to the realization that influences, drives, likes and dislikes, and almost everything that enriches and enlivens human existence, as well as almost everything that can diminish it or impoverish it, have their social context. We do not live *to* ourselves, nor do we live *from* ourselves, although our developing selfhood is so centrally significant for each of us.

Furthermore, in his own developing personality and in his social belonging, man cannot be seen as a purely spiritual creature. He is an "embodied" creature—he has a body; in one sense, as Gabriel Marcel has said, he *is* a body. The popular idea that man is a soul or spirit who happens for a short time to live in a body, from which at death he may be delivered, is preposterous on the face of it, as well as pathetically subchristian and unscriptural. In the old legend found in Genesis, man is made of "the dust of the earth," upon which God has breathed "spirit" so that the dust is animated, given relationships consciously known or deeply felt, and opened to the possibility of a communion not only with other men but also with God himself. But the Bible does not think of man in those highly spiritualized terms which certain strains in Greek thought were concerned to stress; it is a tragedy that so often people who think

23

themselves devoutly Christian lapse into a docetic view of man. Docetism was an early heresy in which the physical side of human existence was rejected as unworthy and unclean; hence, in respect to the person of Jesus Christ, it was claimed that his body was "unreal," only an "appearance" (which is what "docetic" means). The full rich, warm, lived humanity we all know, in which body and mind, sense and spirit, physical and immaterial, are integrated to greater or less fullness in a single existence, is accepted gladly by sound Christian thinkers. It is an egregious error to assume that we are to be and to act as if we were *only* "spirits," for this would be to commit the fallacy which Jacques Maritain has well styled "angelism." Man is *not* an "angel," which by definition of classical theology is "a pure intelligence without body." He is a *man,* which ought to mean that he is a complex organism in which physical and mental, bodily and spiritual, sensible and appreciative or valuational, elements or aspects are so integrated that he is one whole.

This materiality of human life has its obvious connection with man's sexual nature, as we shall see. Unhappily, one consequence of emphasizing the spiritual at the expense of the material in man has been a contempt for, or at best a distrust of, the whole area of human sexuality. Despite the excesses which sometimes manifest themselves, we can therefore be glad that the revolt of contemporary young people against this conventional attitude has taken place. They are not ashamed of their bodies nor are they ashamed of having bodies; they rejoice in these facts. So ought we all to do. It was said of Plotinus, the neo-Platonic philosopher of the early years of our era, that he disliked anybody's referring to his body and that he felt a certain shame in himself possessing one. That refusal to accept the fact of materiality and "embodiedness" led Plotinus, along with other influences, to create a philosophical scheme which is logically argued, in certain respects highly attractive, characterized by insight into human experience as well as by profoundly religious understanding—but basically non-Christian. Anything resembling it should have no place in Christian thinking. It is odd that some Christians, including men of deep faith and serious learning, have tried to be more spiritual than God himself, who presumably created and creates us as embodied creatures because he likes to have us that way.

There are two other points which should be made before this chapter closes. One has to do with the patent and painful fact of man's capacity for choosing wrongly and hence falling into serious defection from the right fulfilment of his personal possibilities. This is what traditionally has been called "sin." The other point is that there is something about human

24

existence which bespeaks "eternal life"—the mortal life which we know is not "enough," we might say, for the restless and dynamic human personality. About each of these points something must now be said.

First, as to defection. Nobody in his senses would think that all human decisions are right ones. Nor would anybody who knows himself and his capacity for self-deception deny that a good deal of the time, men and women seek ends or goals which are not only damaging to others in the total human community but also harmful to themselves. What the word "sin" was devised to express is a patent and terrible fact of human experience.

It would be a mistake, however, to follow certain recent theologians and speak of man's *radical* sin. To say "radical" is to speak of the very roots, the groundwork, of human existence. Thus when these theologians say that man's sin is "radical," they are in fact affirming that in his roots, in the groundwork of his existence, he is in defection from God and hence is thoroughly and completely "bad." But to talk in that way is to deny the great declaration in Genesis, that God's work and the world which he creates are "good." It is also to deny that man is "made in the image of God." On the other hand, to affirm that God's world is "good" and to insist that man is indeed "made in God's image" is *not* to say that there are no distortions in a world "originally" intended to be entirely good, nor that the image of God in man has not been marred and damaged by what men have done during the long course of human history and in their own contemporary life. A balance is needed here between the extremes on the one hand of what sometimes is styled "Augustinianism," which would say that man is *massa corruptionis* ("a mass of corruption") or the "Calvinism" (which Calvin himself does not seem to have held) which regards human existence as "totally depraved," and on the other hand of the easy "Pelagianism" which assumes that man is so good, as he is, that for his proper fulfilment he needs only words of advice and an example of goodness to put him on the road to that fulfilment. The scholastic view that man is indeed basically good, because he is God's child, but that he is *privatus boni et vulneratus in naturalibus* (deprived of a good properly his, namely an open and always "engraced" relation with God, as well as wounded or damaged in his natural qualities of existence), has much to commend it both to sound Christian thought and to intelligent observation of the actual situation. Its defect is that it is usually stated in the context of a static rather than a dynamic view of man's nature.

For ourselves, we may get at the truth by recognizing that the immediately attractive is often easier to choose and apparently more satisfactory to accept. It is to recognize, we might say, that while man must be a self, he can elect to be a self with narrow limits and without adequate regard for the sociality which alone can truly fulfil him. These are "diminishments," in Teilhard's phrase, of human existence. And when they are cumulative, with the long history of the race brought to bear upon the decisions (and consequent actions) of contemporary men, the situation which results is tragic and serious. In classical terms, "man is in sin"— not because he has a body, not because he is sexual, not because he is a creature, but because he and his ancestors have deprived themselves, by choice, of possibilities offered to them. They have rejected again and again the lure to sound fulfilment in which they may realize their potentialities in association with their fellows and so find genuine satisfaction which can be shared "in richest commonalty" with others and with God. This situation, in which we all find ourselves, is such that it requires "redemption"—the setting of men on the *right* path, a change of mind and a re-direction of desire and will. Nor can any man do this for himself; he needs a "helping hand" to give him a new start. The Christian faith affirms that this "helping hand" has in fact been provided: that is the significance of "atonement" or "salvation" wrought out in history by God through Christ. But this is not the place to discuss specific elements in Christian theology. Our present interest is only to say that man may go wrong and that he has gone wrong. The relevance of this "wrong-going" to human sexuality will be indicated as we proceed with our discussion.

Last of all, God "has set eternity" in men's hearts. There is a "beyond" to which men aspire, although (as Bonhoeffer rightly saw) they first meet that "Beyond" (now capitalized because *God* is intended) "in their midst." All the talk about immortality or "life beyond death" and the like has its significance just here. Whatever may be our position in respect to such matters and whether we do or do not subscribe to the view that there is a personal and subjective existence after the death which awaits us all, the *real* point is that only in something more than human, and in that something alone, can man find his genuine fulfilment. That more than human is nothing other than God himself, conceived as the supreme excellence, the utterly perfect, the unfailing Love which "moves the sun and the other stars." Relationship with this, sharing in its purposes, obedience to its summons or lure, and readiness to be an instrument for its continuing action in the world, is man's ultimate happiness, precisely because it is man's final satisfaction. "Thou hast made us to move towards thee, O God," said St. Augustine in a moment of wonderful insight; and he went on to add, "our hearts are in disquietude until they find their true resting-place" (may we not read this to mean "their genuine fulfil-ment"?) "in thee . . ."

How this occurs and what it involves are other matters with which we are not here concerned. But the fact of it, the need for it, and the sense that it is provided somehow for men, seems to me to be essential to a proper understanding of our human existence and to a true perception of what it means to talk about human personality in the making.

Chapter 3
Man's Sexuality

We have seen that man is a personality in the making, with a thrust towards the future fulfilment of his possibilities. He is a living, dynamic, developing creature, possessed of awareness and self-awareness, able to communicate with others, and sharing so profoundly in the human community that he with others forms one common humanity. He is a deciding being, whose choices (however restricted in scope) are made freely and with responsibility as his contribution to the ongoing creative advance. As a body-spirit complex, he is on the way to integration or wholeness.

This is the positive side; on the negative side, as we might put it, he can and observably does make wrong choices which lead to "diminishments" and losses, both for himself and for others. Since he is so profoundly participant in the total existence of the human community, those choices accumulate from generation to generation and have their tragic result in a tendency to selection of immediately available and speciously attractive aims, creating a situation in which lesser goods are so compounded that they become evils. Thus the human race is "in sin," in that its condition is distorted and twisted. The only way out is through new power and the acceptance of "forgiveness," with its futuristic reference:

29

that we shall be treated as and aided towards a development which will overcome wrong-doings in the past by greater opportunities for right-doings in days to come. Now it is in this context that the wrong in man's sexuality is to be understood. The distortions or twistings in human existence are as much expressed through sexuality as anywhere else; we must look at this matter in our seventh chapter. At present our concern is to see exactly what man's sexuality really is and what it involves.

Briefly put, sexuality is the desire and drive to unite oneself with another member of the race, a union which brings enormous satisfaction and which releases energies that otherwise could not find expression. The sexual desire and drive, we are told by many psychologists (especially in the Freudian and neo-Freudian schools) is absolutely central to human existence. This *libido,* which is the urgent activity of man's *eros* or thrust towards union in mutual giving and receiving, is the very heart of his life —or so these experts tell us. I believe that they have got hold of a very important truth and that it is foolish as well as wrongheaded to reject their witness, simply on the grounds that to many they appear to advocate a permissive attitude towards sexual activity.

As these experts talk of it, the sexual nature of man is largely portrayed in terms of emotional responses. But we must remember that man is a physiological as well as a psychological being; his body is as much himself as his desires or his will and reason. Since this is so patently the case, it is extraordinary that so little attention has been paid to the way in which the human body is sexually alive. Not only some of the psychologists but a great many others from many different backgrounds appear to forget the human body when they talk about what it means to be human. Yet the body is obviously *there;* it must be taken most seriously into account when we wish to understand humankind.

The sexual nature of man, then, is inclusive of his physical sexual organs and their rich associations with his entire organism. When a man or woman is excited sexually, the whole body is included in the responses which are made. The most visible manifestation of this, perhaps, may be seen in the human male. Under sexual excitement, his specific sexual organ the penis enlarges and becomes erect. His face may flush. His movements may become spasmodic. He reacts in these visible ways but he also reacts in a less visible manner: the sexual glands become active, the pulse-beat quickens, the "tone" of his bodily feeling changes. Not so obviously but equally profoundly, a woman's response to sexual stimulation brings marked changes in her body. Climactically, both man and woman may be brought to orgasm, in which with uncontrollable but

30

highly pleasurable physical activity extraordinary consequences follow. The ejaculation of semen takes place in the male, while with a woman there is a contraction and expansion which brings delight and satisfaction.

Thus it is apparent that human sexuality has its very definite and essential physical stress. Of course this is something that human beings share with others in the animal kingdom. From the point of view of physical reaction, it might seem that there was little if any difference between the sexual act as performed by two dogs, shall we say, and that performed by two members of the human race. Yet there *is* a difference, about which we must speak shortly—and the difference is such that human sexuality is distinctive and special, despite its similarity (even apparent identity) with sexuality in the animals.

Basically, the sexual desire and drive is deeply instinctive in man. Indeed we might say that a human being without that sexuality would be much less than fully human, as he would also be a very odd specimen of mammal. Furthermore, those who think that they can kill their sexuality, so to say, are fooling themselves. Nature has its way of taking revenge on such people. Even the completely celibate monk has nocturnal emissions, often accompanied by lurid dreams; this is why, in the Compline hymn, the monastics used to pray, in some horror, to be delivered from "pollutions" which seemed to them to be sinful in nature and to be visitations from "the evil one." Women who attempt to trample on their sexuality are likely to be victims of hidden sexual fantasies, often appearing in strange guises. The person who sets out to deny utterly his sexual nature is very frequently the warped "spinster" type—which, as we have observed, seems more frequent in the male than in the female—with an increasingly unpleasant attitude towards others and a serious repression of his own vital powers. This suggests that for those who feel called to a mode of life in which there is no overt sexual expression, the proper attitude is one of glad acceptance of sexuality, coupled with interests and activities that do not so much destroy sexuality—for that cannot happen —as re-direct its expression in other ways. Perhaps all of us have known a few people who have been able to do this.

Yet it is hardly the usual situation. For the vast majority of men and women, *some* expression of sexuality in physical ways is both natural and inevitable. Even if the sexual organs cannot be used in establishing some mode of union with another member of the race, they are almost certain to be used in some fashion—as, for example, in masturbatory activity in the adult where by self-stimulation the sexual organs are brought to the point where satisfaction and release can be obtained.

Not more important than, but intimately associated with, the physical aspect of human sexuality, we are aware of the emotional side. This is physical in the sense that it is both related to and consequent upon glandular activity; yet in another sense, it may be highly imaginative and enjoyed without conscious effort in the strictly physical order. The feeling-tones associated with sexuality are well-known. There is the attraction to another person, the excitation in that person's presence or in thought about him or her, the delight found in being with the one who thus attracts. There is the urge to touch, to caress, to kiss.

It is my own belief that even in friendships which to all intents and purposes are entirely non-sexual, there is this basic emotional quality which is in fact sexual in origin. To some such a thought will appear terrible; they think that their friendships are entirely "pure" and free from any touch of sexuality. But they are mistaken. Intimate male friendships, for example, have a tinge of homosexual attraction; in my judgement, they are not the worse for that. It all depends on whether or not we are prepared to accept our sexual natures and rejoice in them, rather than regard them as something of which we should be ashamed and which at all costs we should seek to hide. Of course this homosexual component in friendships between members of the same sex, along with the heterosexual component in friendships between persons of different sex, is not by any means to be regarded as overt homosexuality in the one case or overt heterosexuality in the other. All I wish to claim is that in human relationships as such, of whatever sort, there is a sexual element precisely because those who are party to them are sexual beings.

The result of sexual congress between man and woman is usually the procreation of a new life. This is the *biological* purpose of the congress—it is the way in which the race is continued. So much we must grant. But there have been times when it has been said that the *only* purpose of sexual relationships was the begetting of children. With the animals, something of the sort may well be the case, although even here some doubt has been expressed by those who have studied animal sexuality. In man, however, the biological purpose, while it may be prior to anything else in terms of historical development in the species, is by no means the main objective in sexual relationships. On the contrary, the main objective seems to be two-fold: First, it is the urge to experience the ecstacy which is felt when humans engage in sexual acts. The pleasure which is obtained is so great that much else will be sacrificed in order to obtain it. In the second place, the objective is the realization of the feeling of union with another human being. This union, in its fullest sense, is a relationship of

32

mutuality, in which through a giving and receiving one from and with the other, two lives are felt to be one. To fail in obtaining that physical union of bodies seems to the partners to be a failure in total union; it is a holding-back or a refusal to give *all* of one's self to the other or a refusal to receive *all* of the other into oneself. Perhaps this is the deep awareness, so deep that it has not always been recognized for what it is, which has brought the Christian tradition to insist that an unconsummated marriage is no marriage at all. In such a marriage, we might say, something has been held back by one partner or the other, or by both in reference to each other, so that the union of lives which marriage entails has not in fact taken place at all.

If we will allow any place at all for sexual relationships of a physical sort between members of the same sex, it is obvious that in such cases the procreation of children is an impossibility. Yet in such cases, the two objectives to which we have just referred are available and are the only possible aims in view. It is likely that the fact that no "third" can be produced in homosexual union explains the condemnatory attitude that has been so commonly felt towards homosexuals; and it is equally likely that one reason for the relaxation of modern people towards homosexuals is precisely the growing awareness that the biological purpose is not the *only* grounds for sexual expression and most certainly not the central objective which is sought. Satisfaction or pleasure, on the one hand, and desire for genuine union of lives, on the other, are much more obviously in view.

We have said that human sexuality must be set in the context of a general portrayal of man such as we presented in the last chapter. It will be useful to see how this works out in practice.

If man is a creaturely "becoming," whose subjective aim is fulfilment of his potentialities with the ultimate end as communion with God, he is also one who finds his proximate end in communion with others of his own kind. This suggests that a relationship with other men and women can and does serve as a means, a sacramental channel, through which ultimate fulfilment in God is both helped and in its degree achieved. Here once again we may appeal to the way in which Christian theology has interpreted the marriage state. It has seen that state as blessed by God; it has also seen it as being a symbol or image, in human affairs, of the fellowship that man is intended to enjoy with his Creator. The analogy of sexual love and of marriage is found time and time again in Holy Scripture both of the Old and New Testaments; and it reaches its highest expression in the image of the Bride of Christ and in the way in which

33

a Jewish love-poem, the *Song of Songs,* has been taken as a description of the human personality in its relationship with God.

Some have thought that this kind of symbolization or imaginative portrayal was illicit, far-fetched, perhaps even absurd. But this is not the case. Something very profound is being said in Christian writing when these pictures are used for this purpose. And if the argument which we are advancing in this book has any truth, we may see that it was inevitable that men, being what they are and experiencing what they do in their sexuality, should speak in just this way. For, as we shall insist in the sequel, the reality of human love which alone is able to bring to actualization the total personality of man is not remote from and in contradiction to divine love. To think in that way would be to denigrate God's creation. And because human love is sexually grounded, the sexual image is more than relevant; it is essential.

In his movement towards actualization, as we have urged, man is not only a personal "becoming"; he is also social—and his "socialization" proceeds *pari passu* with his personalization. Here too his sexuality has its part to play, since it is possible to realize one's sociality only in relationship with *some* others or with *one* other, in some significantly intensive fashion. The intimacy of sexual union, soul and body, sense and spirit, is a focus in which the personal-social quality of man finds expression. Since with that one fellow-human a man is in the closest possible union, the *principle* of human union is established for him. The union with that *one* is particular and special, but it is not utterly exclusive of other associations. Man learns, in his union with one, what is the true meaning of union with all others. This is why no genuine love can be a *jealous* love. As we shall see, faithfulness and commitment to the one is required; yet this does not exclude less intimate, and of course not specifically sexual union, with others of his race.

Furthermore, in sexual relations, when they have reached the level of genuine human quality, there is no mere coupling of bodies but the total bringing-together of personalities in the making—with heart and will, desire and appreciation, as well as physiological functioning, glandular activity, actual insertion or reception of a part of one body into a part of another body. We have here an experience of total self-giving and total other-receiving. I do not know whether this would be conceded by those expert in the various fields of scientific investigation concerned, but it is my own belief that in no experience known to man is complete integration of selfhood so supremely achieved as in the moments of sexual activity. This is not true if we are thinking only of search after sensual grat-

34

ification, although that is not to be despised after the fashion of the "all-too-spiritual" who dislike having bodies. But it seems to me to be profoundly true when the sexual act serves as the expression of genuine love, in which the element of pleasure is included within the urgent desire and drive to give oneself in utter love to another person. Here is an illustration in action of the great saying of Robert Southwell, the recusant poet, whose words I like to quote: "Not where I breathe, but where I love, I live."

"I live," said Southwell . . . and the sort of living of which he is speaking is so inclusive of *all* of the one who loves that sheer joy is experienced, such as the completely whole—that is truly healthy—organism can know. It has been established *as* whole, precisely in the experience of union. Yet it is not a cheap and superficial kind of joy that is known here. For it includes also the anguish which is part of human life. The anguish is overcome, indeed, in the joy which is given; but it is not denied nor destroyed—hence the wisdom of the Spanish proverbial saying that "to make love is to declare one's sorrow." The reason for this ought to be apparent: even in the most intimate of unions, there remains the distinction between selves—otherwise there would not be union but identity, each self having been quite literally denied or destroyed in the oneness which is experienced. But because love is always union, not identity, it is necessary that there be two or more who *are* united; and that distinction can bring a certain pain to any loving spirit.

The linking of man's sexual expression with his awareness of death is also illuminated in this way. When, as in Wagner's *Tristan und Isolde,* love and death are identified, we are in the presence of the wrong kind of understanding of what love is all about. The only sort of death which love demands is death to the purely self-regarding personality; it is not the total death of personality itself. But it is easy to mis-read the experience. It is easy to think that the merging of one with the other equals the death of one with the other; and here perhaps "merging" is precisely the wrong word to use, since it suggests exactly such a death of those participating in loving union. Not merging, then, but *union,* communion, fellowship, mutuality, sharing, entrance of one into the life of the other, symbolized by the entrance of the male penis into the female vagina—here is the proper understanding.

We have already observed that human personality is increasingly communicative of itself. For those who think that communication is best achieved through verbal interchange, the act of sexual union may seem to be less than a supreme mode for such "speaking" one with another.

But I believe that those who think in this way are wrong. Much deeper than words, in my judgement, is that kind of "speech" which is self-expressive without being verbalized, important and necessary as language must be in the establishment of relationships. We all know Wordsworth's phrase about "thoughts that do often lie too deep for tears." Is it not also the case that one human being can communicate with another in actions that no words are adequate either to contain or to express? The union of self with self, when body and mind are together in an association which brings such complete out-pouring of one towards the other, is just such a communication between human beings.

D. H. Lawrence, perhaps more than most other writers of our time, grasped this truth. It would be a mistake to think that Lawrence intended to deny the value of other means of communication; but it was his contention that many sophisticated modern men and women have over-intellectualized, over-rationalized, this capacity to communicate. In consequence they have damaged themselves and distorted their lives. They have lost sight of, or forgotten altogether, the "vitalities" present in their embodied condition as men; thus they have become, not more human because more spiritual, but less human because they tried to be too spiritual. The end-result has been, first, a lofty and unrealistic attitude towards themselves, and second, a strangely and horribly perverted attempt to live on a level to which they do not belong and on which they cannot *really* live. Their existence has been made into a theoretical and abstract effort to avoid what is "natural" to them; they have lost the warmth, the intimacy, the freshness, the enriching quality in their relationships. To cite once again Maritain's word, they are guilty of "angelism" and they suffer for it.

But if men are not angels, neither are they beasts. The reduction of human sexuality to sheer sensuality, after the fashion of the barnyard, overlooks the capacity of man to seek ends, to make evaluations, to appreciate and judge—in all freedom and with all responsibility. This helps us to see why human sexuality is different from that which rightly or wrongly we ascribe to dogs and cats and other animals. Man does not have a "rutting-season" in which he is driven, by the recurrence of period, to engage in sexual activity; he is free to choose the time and the place and the person. To revert to the animal level in sexual matters, as in other aspects of human life, would be to deny manhood. Hence human sexuality, if it is to remain truly human in the context of man's general quality as personality in the making, must be under the control which it is given him to exercise.

Primarily, that control is in terms of love; hence it might be called "love-control." This prepares us for what will be said in the next chapter, in which the meaning of love will be considered. What is important for us to say here, however, is that control by love and in the interests of love is not identical with suppression. The fallacy of the puritan spirit (if that is not to denigrate the Puritans themselves—and here we may doubt whether those who were first given the name ought to be regarded as in fact "puritans" in the pejorative sense) is that it has made precisely this error. Since control of some sort is required in every human life, just because men can make judgements and speak of "better" or "worse" and evaluate the worth of their possible experiences, the puritan spirit assumes that the best way to exercise such control is by the negation of human desire. In another way, some of the popular interpretations of Eastern thought—although quite possibly not the intention of the oriental sages who first spoke in this way—with stress upon the cessation of desire, have suggested that the only way to control man's strong urge is to kill it. Desire is the cause of human suffering and anguish, it is said; therefore it must be altogether suppressed. But this too is a mistake, I believe. What is needed is not a suppression, not a destruction, but a direction and a channeling—briefly, a rightful "ordering" of desire.

St. Augustine saw this when he prayed, in *The Confessions,* that God would "order his loving." Where he too went wrong was when, in violent reaction from what he regarded as the libertinism of his youthful days, he came in his later years to think of human sexuality as the very root of sin. There are some, to us absurd, instances of this kind of thinking in parts of *The City of God*. At the same time, St. Augustine was making an important point. For if human sexuality is intended to be, and can be, the mode through which human personality is given its supremely joyful and right expression, it can also be the mode through which the human tendency to choose immediately available and speciously attractive objectives can be given *its* chief expression. Here St. Augustine sometimes speaks as if he were anticipating what Freud and other modern depth psychologists have told us.

So central in man is his sexuality, his *libido,* his erotic drive, that it stands as the most obvious way in which his real self—this or that human being as he truly is in himself—may be seen. The man who is entirely unable to exercise any control over his sexual desires is the man whose personality is itself uncontrolled. He is tossed to and fro by momentary impulse; he is quite unable to say the necessary "No" at this moment so that the "Yes" at another can be rich and full and glorious.

Here, then, is still another illustration of the way in which human sexual life is set in the wider context of man's existence as a "becoming" person. For the proper fulfilment of man can come about only when he makes decisions which are indeed his own, but which are undertaken in the light of goods greater than those which are immediately obvious and equally immediately attractive. Without the capacity for decision he is not on the way to becoming human; and without the exercise of that capacity in ways that promote his own and the common good, he is denying his emerging manhood and damaging both himself and others. At the same time and by that very token, he is "sinning," since the essence of human sin is to impede the creative advance which is of God and under God. This way of interpreting the meaning of sin is not the conventional one, to be sure. But I believe it to be the sound and right way, in the light of all that we know about ourselves as emerging personalities in a cosmic process marked by the "creative advance" of which I have spoken. Certainly it is not a minimizing of the tragedy and the horror of sin, even if it is a different interpretation of that tragedy and horror.

Man can and does sin, in his sexual life. Not in that life exclusively, of course, but in that life in a signal and obvious manner, he fails in control and he fails in the right sort of selectivity. Hence the possibility of distortion and twisting, which we might describe as deviation from the routing or direction which is given him with his "initial aim" and to fulfil which is his supreme subjective aim. But when he seeks, in all responsibility, to "order" his life by love and in the service of love, he is moving in the direction which is proper to him. His sexual desire and drive is then expressed in ways that contribute to his healthy development and they are in accord with the "will of God"—which will is nothing other and nothing less than that man shall become genuinely and rightly human.

Chapter 4
Love and Sexual Expression

In closing the last chapter, we saw that in human personality the reality of love is the deepest and truest significance of human sexuality. Why, it may be asked, was not this point made *before* anything else was said about sexual desires and drives? The answer is that I wished at all costs to avoid suggesting to the reader a too spiritual, too ethereal, view of the meaning of love; I wished to ground it in the sexuality which is so central to human personality, rather than let it float in some empyrean which would be above and even remote from the actual world of human experience.

Altogether too often, as it seems to me, precisely this has been the mistake of those who speak about love. They talk about it as if it were something so "ideal" that it does not come into contact with human life as it is known by men in their concrete day-by-day existence. Indeed one might say that much that is written or said about love would suggest that it is an "ideal form," in the Platonic sense, to which men come when they have passed entirely beyond the ordinary world of experience. This approach is hardly Plato's own, since in the *Symposium* we find him beginning with the way in which human beings fall in love with beautiful or attractive bodies and then, as he sees it, rise through a series of levels to the contemplation of love in itself—although, even there, there is much in Plato to suggest that he was not anything like so "idealistic," in the common meaning of that term, as some "Platonists" have tended to assume.

In any event, whatever may have been the case with the great Greek thinker, the plain fact is that nobody in ordinary experience encounters "love" in the abstract. Like all human awareness of "values" or "forms," these are known to us in their embodiments; perhaps this quasi-Aristotelean emphasis is a necessary corrective to the type of interpretation of Plato's thought which has spoken of "values" *apart from,* rather than *in,* that which in fact men do experience.

For a Christian, whose world-view is determined by the position taken in the Jewish-Christian Scriptures, a retreat from the world or an effort to extricate oneself from worldly involvements ought to be completely impossible. The Jewish attitude is very worldly indeed, in the sense that it focuses attention on the actual world in which human personality is set—whatever may be said about God or spirit, about heaven or hell, about anything that is "spiritual," is always related to and derived from the concrete actuality of the here-and-now. When the Jew talked about God, for example, he did not do this in such a fashion that God was pictured apart from his activity in the world of nature and history. The Jew appeared to have had little if any interest in an abstract deity. Jahweh was known in and through his world; he was at work in and revealed through the course of nature and the events of history. He was seen in the things that happened to men. He was God-in-relation-with-the-world, not God in utter separation from that world. This did not mean that there was no distinction between God and world. Whatever else a Jew might be, he was never pantheistic in attitude. But neither was he a deist whose God was utterly remote from the creation, once he had got it going. God and world were inseparable in his thinking, yet they were not the same thing—although he would never have phrased it this way, the Jew was well aware of what a logician might style the difference between the connotations of the words "separation" and "distinction."

Furthermore, in Christian thought the faith in Jesus Christ as the incarnation of God in the concrete events of history and human life has led to a recognition of the divine involvement in the affairs of the world. Not only in the Incarnate Lord himself, but in the whole course of God's working in the creation, there is both a distinction between divine and creaturely and also a denial of any separation of the divine from the creaturely. The incarnational principle has led also to the sacramental

40

principle; here the eucharistic action, where material things (bread and wine) are the agency in and through which God makes available the continuing presence through action of his incarnate Son, is seen as providing a clue to the way in which elsewhere and otherwise God also works in the world.

The "love of God," or "God as love," must for Christians always be qualified by the further phrase, "in Christ Jesus our Lord"; and by extension, whatever is said about God is always said about him in consequence of what has been known or experienced or apprehended or felt in the doing of God in the creation. And this ought to require the Christian to see that when he wishes to speak of love in a more general sense, and indeed of any other "value" such as goodness or beauty or truth or justice, he must speak of it *as he knows it*—which is to say, in its embodied manifestation. Nobody has ever seen pure truth, but all of us have known, perhaps, statements or propositions which are true; nobody has seen sheer beauty in and of itself, but we have been captured by beautiful forms or representations, whose harmony appeals to us and secures our grateful response. Goodness, too, is known in good men, good deeds, good thoughts and words.

Hence both common sense and Christian thought have to start from the place where we are, the things that we know, and the experiences that we have. Which is only another way of insisting, with St. Thomas Aquinas, that whatever we know is known to us *ad modum recipientis*—according to the human capacity to understand, appreciate, and accept. Thus there is a sound theoretical as well as a natural human requirement that a discussion of love should be preceded by a discussion of the human "equipment," as we might call it, through which men and women do, as a matter of fact, come to know what that love is all about.

But what *is* love?

Here once again we should be careful to avoid the peril of an overly "spiritual" interpretation. Or perhaps I should have said, "an overly sentimental" way of thinking about love—for oddly enough, the two, spiritual over-emphasis and sentimental absurdity, very frequently go together. In any case, it is a grave mistake to think that love is only a sort of niceness which has little if any connection with the hard and sometimes harsh realities of life in this world. At the same time, however, it is a mistake to speak of love (as some thinkers, in reaction from sentimentalism, have done) as if it were not in any sense an affair of the emotions but entirely a matter of the direction of the will. Love is not identical with "liking," but it is related to it; and one is dismayed sometimes by

41

those who can say something like, "I love but I don't like . . ." That seems, to me anyway, to border on the inhuman, as it certainly borders on the inhumane.

A phenomenology of love is therefore necessary. In another book I have sought to speak of this matter in a popular vein (*Love Looks Deep*, Mowbrays, 1969); here I should like to point out several elements or aspects of love which are relevant to our present topic. The ingredients of love, I believe, include at least the following: commitment or dedication; the desire to give to another from the deepest levels of oneself; the willingness to receive from another that which he or she would give; expectation of fresh and refreshing novelty in the relationship of one human being with another; union or communion or fellowship or sharing. And all these add up to fulfilment, in which each person finds himself on the way to becoming more genuinely a human being, his personality growing and expanding as it discovers in the other that which elicits the realization of the possibilities which are present and available for each. It will be observed that these characteristics of love are related to what was said in the last chapter about human sexuality in its finest expression. Naturally this relationship holds, since (as we have argued) the sexuality of man is the natural and human grounding for his awareness of love in all its beauty and appeal. We should rejoice in this relationship rather than think of it as unfortunate or degrading. The point is that human sexuality must be seen in the light of the significance we find in love, not that love is to be "reduced" to the level of merely animal sexuality. Here again we perceive the difference between the sexual in man and the sexual which we see (or think we see, anyway) among the animals who do not possess that valuational and appreciative, deciding and responsible, capacity which is found in human personality.

Commitment or dedication is an essential element in the meaning of love. To commit oneself to another means to entrust oneself to that other one's whole being. Here the stress must fall on the two words "entrust" and "whole." The opposite of genuine commitment is a failure to give, in the sense of offering to the other what one is and has so that the other may take this and use this—but use it, in genuine loving, for the relationship itself rather than for his own ends. When I say that I "trust" someone, I am saying that I have complete confidence in him, certain that what he does and is will never "let me down." And when I "entrust" myself to another, I am saying that I put myself in the other's hands, sure that in those hands I am ultimately entirely *safe,* precisely because the other is known to be "trustworthy." Yet it is not quite correct to say that the other

42

is "known" to be such, for that might suggest that I have some logical proof that such is the case. On the contrary, the situation is much more venturesome. For what I am doing is giving myself into the other's hands in a great act of faith; I do not *know* in any demonstrable fashion that he is what I take him to be. I cannot prove to you that someone to whom in love I thus entrust myself is in very fact what I am confident he is.

This is what gives to love its "dangerous" quality, since it is always a risk to give oneself to another without rationally demonstrated certainty. Yet love demands this, requires this, entails this giving of self. And it is a giving of the *whole* self, too, with nothing held back. The person who seeks to keep for himself one bit of his life—this or that special area—is not the true lover; he is altogether too cautious to be that. Love is *not* cautious; it is, as one might put it, careless in self-giving. I have already noted that, in such commitment as love entails, the total personality is offered to the other—and in the normal instance, this is body as well as mind, for the *whole* self includes both. And when the love is such that it includes the actual and physical giving of one's body, we have to do with sexuality in its strict significance. Yet even when there is not that actual physical giving, one's body is also involved in the commitment, precisely because we are body-mind entities. There are other ways than the sexual act, in whatever fashion we envisage this, for the giving of body to another. It may be only the willingness to touch and be touched; it may be even less than that—perhaps it is just the necessity of our being bodies at all that is offered. However that may be, the commitment is complete, with nothing held back.

This desire to give is from the very depths of one's selfhood. Here is the second element which I have noted. A superficial sort of giving will not do, when love is in the picture. Obviously this is a variation on the theme we have just been discussing; nonetheless, it is important to notice its significance. There are relationships, good enough in themselves, in which we are not moved to the very bottom of our existence nor feel moved to give from such depths. These acquaintanceships, as I have suggested elsewhere (in *Love Looks Deep*), are of the order of the "I-You," not of the "I-Thou"—if we may adapt here the language used by Martin Buber. They are most certainly not "I-It" relationships, appropriate to *things* and, in certain connections where absolutely no personal involvement of any sort appears to be required, with those with whom we can have but a remote and (so to say) "official" contact. But when it is a matter of love, the desire is to open oneself fully to the other. As nothing is held back, so nothing is hidden. Everything is given, everything is revealed. I am willing to be and I want to be entirely naked before the one I love.

The next point is perhaps more controversial. It has to do with the willingness to receive that which the other wishes to give to me. The reason that this is controversial finds its explanation in the theory of love which has been advocated by some contemporary theologians and also by some who have written about the literary revelations of love in human affairs. These have urged that between love as self-giving, which they call by the Greek word *agape,* and love as willingness and even desire to receive, which they call *eros,* there is a great chasm. True love, such as God has for his creatures, must be pure *agape,* they say. In it there is no urge to receive, since for them that would destroy the very purity which they believe characterizes such love. On the other hand, in ordinary love such as men and women may know between themselves, there is an element of impure *eros*—or if not impure, certainly less than perfect. Now I believe that this sort of thinking is as inhumane and as untrue psychologically as it is disastrous theologically. I am *not* saying, mind you, that the condition for loving, in terms of commitment of the whole self to another, is that I shall receive from the other; I am only saying that there is the *willingness* to receive, even the *desire* to receive, whatever the other wishes to give. Far from being an easy sort of "I give so that I may get" attitude, as some appear to assume, this willingness and desire is very difficult indeed. Someone has remarked that it is much harder to accept from another than it is to give to another. That may be too extreme; yet I am convinced that when we analyze our own feelings, we find that the business of receiving is *not* easy. For to receive, to be willing to receive, to desire to receive, is by way of admitting that we *need* to receive; it is a confession of one's own inadequacy. And that is not an easy confession for any man to make, since pride always dogs us and we should like to think that we are sufficient unto ourselves.

This, I take it, is why genuine love is the very opposite of pride and the self-sufficiency which goes with it. In love we *admit* our personal poverty and see ourselves as we really are—imperfect, inadequate, in need of what others can provide for us and give to us. Hence we are willing to receive, glad to receive, desirous of receiving, what the one who loves us is glad to give. Our pride is humbled, our self-sufficiency seen as absurd. Or to repeat an earlier phrase, we know ourselves and reveal ourselves in all our nakedness and with all our want.

Fourth, part of loving is expectation. Here I am not talking about a sort of wistful hope that "something good will turn up somehow or other."

On the contrary I am speaking of that eager attitude which recognizes the inexhaustible possibilities in another person and rejoices in the expectation that in the relationship which we enjoy with that other there will emerge splendid novelties, unexpected in the ordinary sense of that word. When the poet Hopkins, speaking of the cosmos as a whole, says that "there lives the dearest freshness deep down things," one may extend his phrase to include the "dearest freshness" which lives "deep down" in the person loved; from that profound source, we confidently expect, there will emerge manifestations that are indeed fresh and wonderful. Human life in love is not a matter of deadly monotony, although there are the long stretches during which novelty does not appear. Life in love is various, surprising, enriching, because one is never able to predict just what will emerge nor when it will emerge. Hence there is a delight in love at its best, answering to that aspect of human experience which insists that life shall *not* be on one level but shall be compounded of "ups" and "downs," with genuine surprises that make us, as we are prone to say, "sit up and take notice."

What is more, this "expecting" attitude in love is a means for awakening in the other his capacity *to be* surprising. If nothing much is expected, nothing much is likely to occur; but if those who love do expect great and novel things, the likelihood is that they will happen. Somebody has humorously remarked that for many rather humdrum people there is "another beatitude": "Blessed are those who expect nothing, for they shall not be disappointed." Precisely so, although "blessed" is hardly the proper word to characterize such persons. If we are honest, we shall be obliged to admit that the right description would rather be, "cursed" or perhaps (in a weaker but more accurate word) "miserable." The truly "blessed"—which, we may recall, is a translation of *makarios,* the Greek word whose meaning is "happy"—are those who *because* they expect great things, are *not* disappointed, since their expectation arouses, stimulates, lures, entices, from the other the response which he may give.

Next, and finally, we come to union or communion or fellowship. All these terms suggest mutuality or sharing or participation of one life with another life. Here we have to do with something that is central to the meaning of love. In the commitment of self to self, in the giving to a self who also gives, in the opening of personality to another personality, in the eager expectation of great things from that other, there is established a sharing of human life which brings the deep fellowship after which all men yearn and without which they feel that their existence is drab and pointless. William Morris once said that fellowship is heaven and lack of fellowship is hell. I believe that this is profoundly true. Man was not made to be alone, although there is a certain solitariness about his existence which cannot be denied. Yet that solitariness exists only to be shared with another person and with other persons. To be "at one" with another, in union with him at every level of selfhood, is to be truly and really on the way to becoming a person. Hence, as we noted at the end of our list of love's ingredients, fulfilment is to be found in love and nowhere else.

Now it is apparent that human beings, as personalities in the making, do not arrive at the complete expression of the several elements I have listed. They do not give themselves in complete commitment; they do not desire to have their depths known nakedly to others; they do not find it easy to receive from another; they are often lacking in expectation; and they do not achieve or discover the union which will fulfil them. Which is only another way of observing that we are indeed personalities *in the making* who have not yet arrived at our intended destination. But the important question is whether we are *on the way there,* not whether we have in fact arrived. In any judgements we may make about ourselves and others, this is the question to ask. Thus we shall be preserved from the absurd claim that everything is achieved and that we are "all right," while at the same time we may encourage ourselves and others by considering the direction which is being followed. Kindlier and more accurate judgement is then made possible for us. On ourselves, to be sure, we may make the more severe judgement, since we know better than anyone else the degree of our failure and, if we examine ourselves, some of the reasons for it. So far as others are concerned, we are prepared to "make allowances," however; and thus to "make allowances" is not to be slipshod or easy-going but to be understanding and discerning in our evaluation.

What this amounts to is plain enough. It has already been hinted in what was said earlier about man's more general nature—namely, that he is a creature of such a sort that only an "eternal" satisfaction will truly bring him the full realization of his potentialities. As we said at that point, this is what talk about "heaven" (and for that matter "hell") really signifies in an existential awareness such as can always be ours. The incompleteness and imperfection which we see in ourselves and discover in others is a sign of our continuing movement towards the fulfilment which is possible only "in God." There alone, as St. Augustine observed in the words which we quoted from *The Confessions,* can "our restless" or "unquiet" hearts find their true rest and quietude. This is the abiding "eschatological" note in all genuinely human living. Were it not so, man would be less than man; he would be living, or trying to live, on what we often style "the animal level"—although that may be unfair to the animals! Man's thrust towards the future, his *pour-soi* (if one may adopt a Sartrian phrase), discloses itself in his sense of imperfection in the here-and-now and in his yearning for a fulfilment which nothing in this world can give, not even the deepest and most gloriously enriching love of another human being. On the other hand, it is through such loving that he also discloses that he is indeed moving towards that fulfilment, since God has so ordered his creation that our human loving is the surrogate, the sacramental sign and instrument, the *arrabon* or partial presence, of that end or goal which perfectly and completely provides fulfilment. And notice that in the traditional portrayals of "heaven," we are shown both the "vision of God" *and* the "communion of saints." Fulfilment is never enjoyed by each man in and for and of himself; it is in commonalty, shared in a fellowship in which each one is related, in the most intimate manner, with others, while all are enfolded in the love which is God himself. In the Epistle to the Hebrews, we are told by the writer (after he has given his catalogue of the "witnesses") that we *apart from them* shall not be made perfect. Here is a penetrating insight into the human condition, both in its present incomplete stage and in its final completion—we were made for each other, we live with one another, we help one another, and without the others we cannot ourselves come to whatever fulfilment is intended for us.

Before we end this chapter, there is one further point to be made. It is a simple, almost an obvious one, yet it is often forgotten. Love is always a *gift;* it is never something which a man can "earn" by his efforts. That is the point, but it must not be misunderstood. For there is a paradox here. While love *is* a gift, it requires everything that a man can have and do if he is to receive the gift. Yet what is required is by way of *response,* calling forth from us all our strength and demanding that we shall labour on behalf of the beloved. The *gift* is paramount, however. That is why in popular songs we are told about how one "falls in love" or how love "happens" when we least expect it. They may exaggerate, of course, but they do not exaggerate beyond all reason. The truth is that we find ourselves loved, or we find ourselves loving—we do not "work ourselves up" to the state in which we love or are loved. We can put ourselves in the way of love, by being open and friendly with others; we can "prepare and make ready" the path of love. But none of this will bring love to us. For it is "of grace," as theology would say; it is free gift and freely-bestowed favour, which is what the theological word "grace" means to say.

I return now to my earlier insistence that what has been said about love is grounded, naturally and physically, in the sexual desire and drive in man. And I repeat that this is nothing of which we need be ashamed, nor is it something which calls in question the nobility and wonder of love itself. We need, once and for all, to eradicate from our minds and to dismiss from our thought the strangely pervasive idea that physical conditioning—in this case, sexual existence with its physiological factors —is something that is either evil or at best "not quite nice."

Perhaps I can best make the point here by recounting a little incident. A young man once said that he was greatly distressed by the fact that when he saw the girl whom he loved, he had a disturbing physical reaction—to put it bluntly, he was aware, on such occasions, of some slight stiffening of his sexual member. This troubled him, for he knew that his love was both genuine and, as he put it, "entirely pure." What was one to say to him? My own response was to say that he should be *glad* of what happened; for after all, was he not a complete male, equipped with the organs and senses proper to one of his own sex? And was it not a sign that in his love of that girl, *all* of him was included, his emotions and his will, his mind and his heart, *and* also his body? In his relations with the girl he loved, he would naturally wish to act in a manner that showed his respect for her, his desire to express himself physically only in the way that was pleasing to her, and in full sexual union only when their loving relationship had been established and was known for what it meant—in his case and with his convictions, this permitted no full sexual intercourse until marriage. *But* as a total male personality, the physical reaction that troubled him was a good thing, not a bad one.

Chapter 5
The Heterosexual Expression of Sexuality

For the great majority of men and women, the usual expression of their sexuality is through relations with persons of the opposite sex to their own. "Boy meets girl, boy falls in love with girl, boy marries girl"—so the saying has it; and there can be no doubt that most people would agree with what it is telling us. On the other hand, there are some men and women who feel a sexual attraction to members of their own sex; these are the homosexuals, whether their expression of sexual desire and drive is overtly or latently active. Until fairly recently persons of this kind were considered to be evil, certainly abnormal and unnatural in their feelings, and if not criminals surely sinners. Nowadays, for a great many reasons, the attitude towards them has altered and they are much more likely to be accepted by society. In the following chapter, the homosexual expression of human sexuality will be considered, with a sympathy equal to that shown to the heterosexual; the present chapter is devoted to the sexuality of the vast majority of human beings, expressed as it is through heterosexual relationships.

The first point to which reference must be made may seem very remote from our subject, if not in actual contradiction to it. This is the matter of human chastity. Commonly this word has been taken to mean complete sexual abstinence and has therefore been identified with celibacy. But the true meaning of chastity is, or ought to be, sexual life according to the right ordering of human nature—as a Christian would say, in accordance with God's plan and purpose for humanity. The chaste person is not necessarily one who remains unmarried. He is one who is in control of the physical and external expression of his sexuality, so that the sexual drives may be used in the best possible way as an expression of genuine love—love in the sense in which we described it in the preceding chapter. In other words, the chaste man or woman is the one who recognizes that his sexual expression is to be enjoyed; but it is to be seen not as an end in itself, as if man were simply a sexual being and nothing else. It is regarded as a central and splendid means for bringing love into all our relationships, for serving God and serving our fellowmen, and for actualizing in a concrete act the union of one personality with another. It is precisely for this reason that the faithfulness, mutuality, and sharing to which we have referred are essential elements in the relationship of person with person, when this is not reduced to the level of sensual gratification without regard for others. The distinction between love and animal lust may be seen just here. There is absolutely nothing wrong about lust, if this means the urgent sexual instinct in man; but it can *become* wrong when it is entirely out of context. When it is *in* context, however, it is good—and then it is a component in the total thrust of human love. The truly chaste person is the person whose sexuality is thus in context, under control by love, with tenderness and full awareness of the other with whom he wishes to be united.

Marriage of man and woman is the usual way in which this relationship is known. And whatever may have been the case with more primitive peoples, where indeed the evidence is bewildering and no definite conclusions can be drawn, in the more advanced or civilized nations and peoples the idea of marriage is associated with monogamous relationships. One man and one woman are united in a bond which is given social approval; some ceremony or rite, usually a religious one, announces the intention of the couple to live together as man and wife, and they are accepted as such by the other members of their tribe or community. The responsibilities which this entails differ greatly from place to place and from time to time, as do the customs and usages associated with the married state; but that there *are* responsibilities seems clear in every case known to us. The result is the establishment of a family, for sooner or

50

later there will be children (in most cases, at least). There is thus an inner grouping, with man and wife and children forming a nucleus whose purpose is the mutual support and help provided by all for each and by each for all.

The uniting of man and woman in marriage has made possible an approved way to develop those qualities of love upon which we have insisted. The commitment or dedication, the giving-and-receiving relationship, the mutuality, etc., are all given a setting which makes it much easier for people to grow in them towards fulfilment. That fulfilment is with a person of one's own kind, but of another sex. There is opportunity for faithfulness and tenderness one with another. Sexuality so conceived has been raised by Christian instinct to the level of a sacrament of the church. This was not by accident. By some deep insight the Christian church saw how such a sexual relationship could be, and was, a token of God's presence as Love. He is "the third" who binds the couple into one life. The estate of marriage becomes both a sign of God's action in the world and a way in which the reality of that action may be grasped and appreciated, however feebly and imperfectly, by his human children.

It is hardly necessary to note that the usual consequence of sexual union in which a man and a woman enter into bodily contact, with all its physiological implications, is the conception and birth of another being. But sometimes the fact, so well known, and the depths of meaning in human sexuality, are not rightly related one to the other. The clue to the relationship is found in the word most frequently used to describe it: procreation. *Pro*-creation: creation on behalf of an Other, namely God. The relationship of sexual union to the conception of another human life is simply, though very mysteriously, the fruitfulness or fecundity of love. And if love be *of* God, since he *is* Love, then this fruitfulness or fecundity is a manifestation of the quality of the divine Charity as men may share it. What might have been taken only as a biological consequence of the sexual act may now be recognized as something even deeper than that, although inevitably inclusive of that. Not that reproduction is the whole meaning of sexual union, for as we have already indicated that is not the case. But in the great majority of instances, even when the human partners rightly desire to exercise some control over the number and spacing of their offspring—hence "family control" is a better term here than "contraception"—one or more children will be born to the couple who in heterosexual relations have entered upon the married state. So superabundant is their love, reflecting as it does the overflowing and diffusive love which is of God, that it cannot be content with mutuality

51

alone; it seeks new and unexplored areas in which it may be manifested. It creates, under God, another human life—not by biological accident as with animals, but because in itself it is a creative thing which enriches those who share it and which through that enrichment would diffuse itself more widely. Having thus created life, it provides opportunity for further manifestation in a family where love may work effectively upon the young. Thus the basic animal or biological fact of reproduction is taken up into the context of self-giving love, love which also receives, and which is diffusive of itself after the pattern and in the power of the divine Love from which it has its ultimate source and to which it finally returns.

Since this book is not a text-book in sexual behaviour or practices, it is hardly necessary to discuss either the kinds of activity in which men and women engage, in physical relations, or the adjustments which they must make one to the other in respect to the times, the frequency, and the occasions in which such activity takes place. But it *is* important to notice that the wisdom of the Christian centuries has seen that without consummation a marriage cannot be regarded as complete and real. Hence failure to consummate a marriage in sexual union is one of the accepted grounds for annulment. Now this points clearly to the centrality of the sexual act in the marriage relationship. And the reason is not that without such union, the marriage will be without offspring. Much more profoundly, I believe, the reason is that Christian insight has been penetrating enough to recognize that a full union, a giving of oneself entirely to another self who gives in return, must of necessity include the body as well as the mind. Thus we are back once again to the point that man is an organic whole, whose bodily nature is just as truly a part of him as his rationality or his capacity for spiritual contacts.

The understanding of marriage in lands that have been exposed to Christian influence is that it is life-long, not subject to rupture whenever one party happens to feel a little bored or tired of the other. Here we have a reflection of love as entailing commitment or dedication. It was Gabriel Marcel, I believe, who once said that one of the unique things about men is that they can and do *make promises*—the world in which they live is of the sort that permits, even demands, promise-making, while those who make them are able to intend to fulfil them. But a promise, when it is made in the context of heterosexual love, can only signify genuine commitment when it is "for always." "Till death do us part," says the marriage service. Those words pay a very high tribute to the persons who take them upon their lips; they bespeak the possibility of unceasing attachment to and concern for another, "for better for worse, for richer for poorer, in sickness and in health," as the service goes on to say. And the phrases are followed by the other words, "to love and to cherish." Loving and cherishing: there is the self-giving, the mutuality, the willingness to receive, of which we have spoken; there too is the tenderness ("to cherish") which is the mark of love at its noblest.

Now tenderness between a man and a woman does not mean sentimentality or a policy of senseless *laissez-faire*. Genuine tenderness is compounded of gentleness and strength—gentleness, in that there is no coercion or pressure, no attempt to force the other into agreement or into conformity with one's own likes and dislikes, tastes and antipathies; and strength in that there is in each partner the retention of the full integrity of his own self. The weak cannot be tender in this sense; the *overly*-strong (that is the self-assertive and domineering) cannot be tender either. Marriage is a school in which tenderness is first intended and then by daily practice becomes part of personality's developing pattern.

In the early days of marriage, the specifically physical side may loom very large indeed; and rightly so, since the vigour of youth as well as the sheer attraction of the other's body is so much in the picture. As a couple lives together, the physical does not become unimportant, as some have claimed. What does happen is that the physical becomes more and more part of a developing order or patterning of life. It ought never to become an automatic or mechanical or stereotyped affair; but it can certainly become less demanding. Yet we should not assume that it is any the less important. And in more subtle ways, human sexuality is still present and active—perhaps for times only in the delight of the man and wife in simply being together. Being together is a bodily matter, it must be remembered; there is physical propinquity, even when there is not actual sexual union. In old age, the physical side cannot be so frequently enjoyed, if it can be enjoyed at all; although here modern study has shown that the supposed complete loss of specifically physical desire is very largely a myth. The couple have so grown into each other, so deeply belong one to the other, that the lessening of urgent sexual drives does not seriously damage their relationship.

As we are well aware, in the sexual act it is the man who penetrates the woman and the woman who receives the man. This symbolizes or signalizes the difference between them. It should not be interpreted to mean that the male is the aggressive partner while the woman is the passive and merely accepting one. Very often this is not the case; it is the woman who, so to say, makes the approaches to her husband. But what is indicated by the physiological facts in the sexual act ought to be clear

53

enough. The male, precisely because of his more obviously active role, requires the tempering and "gentling" which will reduce masculine aggressiveness; the woman, because she is the recipient in the sexual act, needs on her part to acquire something of the energetic activity which characterizes her husband. They can both be helped in making their personalities by acquiring from the other member that which appears to be less developed in themselves.

So once again the married state is shown to be a school in which men and women learn how to love. But what can be said of heterosexual relationships before marriage? And what can be said about them when they are sought with other persons than the marriage partner?

As to the latter, I believe that the wisdom of the Christian tradition is very much to the point here. Normally such relationships are to be discouraged, at least when they come to the point where actual sexual contacts are in view. This is not because sex is an evil thing; it is simply because the promises made one to the other, the commitment or dedication which love entails, rule out the possibility of one partner's being able to give himself or herself in any genuine completeness to another person. We may be able to understand, even to sympathize with, a wife who feels drawn to another man, when her husband is cold and unable or unwilling to respond to her urgent desire for his love. But we need not permit this understanding and sympathy to allow us to accept disloyalty as a good thing. So also in respect to the male partner. It is in such cases that the reality of control by love is so significant. Adultery, whether in the full physical sense or in some attenuated meaning of the term, is not an attractive thing—and it is damaging not only to the "innocent" party but also to the "guilty" one, since it implies the breaking of an originally intended faithfulness on the latter's part.

When we come to pre-marital sexuality, the situation is rather different. Everybody is familiar with the fact that young people are likely to wish to engage in what is called sexual experimentation. There is nothing evil about the desire, as such. The problem is essentially one of respect and genuine personal concern. The young man who is out to "make" every girl he meets shows scant respect for those victims of his desires, nor does he have much if any concern for their personal integrity. Yet there can be occasions when a boy and girl genuinely feel a deep affection for each other and wish to cement that affection by physical relationships. Condemnation is easy here, especially by older persons in whom the sexual urge is less strong. What is required is an awareness of the strength of the pressure felt by one or both of the parties, with a recognition that there can be cases where love, or what is honestly thought to be love, almost demands the physical act. No rules can be laid down, especially in a day when "petting," in various degrees of intimacy, is taken for granted by our culture. But it can be said that no young boy should wish to take advantage of another human being, unless and until the other is also ready and willing, while no young girl should easily let herself be put in the position where she cannot refuse consent precisely because she has either "led on" her friend or has allowed him to proceed, stage by stage, to the point at which there is no holding-back.

One can see, however, that a good deal of the criticism of the prevalent sexual freedom among younger people rests upon either too spiritual a view of human sexuality *or,* on the opposite side, a too cheap view of physical sex. In the former case, the attitude assumes that love is so much a matter of the ideal world that it has no bodily factors—and this is unrealistic as well as absurd. In the latter case, the sexuality in man has been degraded to the animal level and its setting in man's total personality has been forgotten. Then sexual relationships have no more meaning than the coupling of dogs in heat. As we have argued earlier in this book, the specific differentia in human sexuality are found precisely in those elements or factors of faithful commitment, giving-and-receiving, mutuality, hopefulness, union of total personality, etc., all coupled with the tenderness which combines gentleness with strength. Without these, sexuality is indeed an expression of animal drives, rather than an expression of human desires. But man is not meant to live, and at his best knows that he cannot happily live, on the merely animal level, any more than he can do this on the angelic or purely spiritual level.

It was G. K. Chesterton who once said that while one cannot meaningfully tell a crocodile, "Be a crocodile," one *can* meaningfully tell a man, "Be a man." After all, the crocodile is being a crocodile to the limit of his potential "crocodility"; but because man is "in the making," he is never a man to the limit of his possible personal manhood. If it be the purpose of God that every human being should be on the way to becoming, in the complete sense, a personality in community with others, then it makes sense to ask that each man shall realize this and shall lend all his energies, both in self-control and in self-expression, so that his goal may be achieved. This has an obvious bearing upon human sexuality, as upon other and less central aspects of his manhood.

Something should now be said about the heterosexual male or female who for some reason does not marry. This failure to take a life-partner may be because of a sense of vocation to some specific kind of task—as,

55

for example, in the monk or the nun. It may be because "Mr. Right" has not come along for the woman, or "the girl I truly love" has not been met by the man. Or it may be because there is some impediment, not in sexual drive (as would be the case with the homosexual, to whose situation we shall soon give attention) but in interest or even in physical make-up, which prevents the attempt at marriage.

Now the one thing that needs to be said about all these cases is that they do not involve the non-sexualization of the persons in question. Even with the monk and the nun, the heart of the matter is not really the destruction of the sexual desires and drives; rather, it is the re-direction of them in terms of the specific vocation which has been chosen. Here nobody can judge another. To many the "religious life" will seem senseless, of course; but there are others to whom it is far from sense-less, but instead is the response to a call which to them is so compelling that they cannot fail to answer it positively. Such persons need to channel their sexuality in such a way that without its destruction it can be directed to ends that have a wider and less physical expression. So also, in appropriate ways, with those who either cannot marry or who are unable to find the person with whom, as they think, a life-long relationship might be established.

Religious faith, when it is not mere escapism, can be of enormous help in all these cases. Obviously it is so, in respect to the "religious," the monks and nuns. But it can also aid others. It may seem too easy to say it, but observation confirms the fact that the celibate state can be dedicated to the service of other persons, in ways appropriate to their condition and circumstances; in and through their willingness to care for and show concern about other persons, as well as about compelling causes or objectives, the celibate can be more or less consciously dedicated to the divine Lover whom we call God. To realize this possibility and to act upon it can remove much, if not all, of the sting which so often is felt by the unmarried. Some, if not all, of their loneliness can be relieved; and they can bring themselves to accept the remainder with cheerfulness and not in spiteful despair. Indeed, some of the "sweetest" persons one comes to know are those who have done precisely this. The danger, of course, is that they will *not* will such dedication to others and such acceptance of their situation; then, alas, they are all too likely to become "spinsters," in the pejorative meaning of that word. They may be embittered, spiteful, disagreeable, grudging in attitude, uncharitable and unkind to others. Perhaps there is no more pathetic spectacle in the world of human affairs than the man or woman (more often, one thinks, the man) who lets himself become a "spinster" and in so doing is an unpleasant companion to those who must meet him.

In concluding this chapter, it will be well to return to the opening discussion. There we saw that for the great majority of men and women, the "normal" expression of sexuality is achieved through the establishment of a marriage relationship. They are heterosexuals, whose sexual attraction is to a person of the opposite sex. In Christian thought, this relationship is said to be grounded in the divine purpose: "Male and female created he them." And in Christian thought, marriage is itself divinely instituted. This does not mean that there was some voice from on high which announced the validity of marriage; man has come to understand marriage from primitive beginnings, rooted even before human beings emerged in the biological realm. From polygamy and polyandry, from earlier conceptions of sexual activity and its meaning, there has emerged the typical civilized position that monogamous marriage is the proper, the usual, and in certain ways, the "normal" and "natural" state for man. Informed Christian theologians know perfectly well that this has been a progressive deepening of understanding about how to secure a rightful and enriching manifestation of those drives which men originally shared with the animal kingdom.

What is distinctive in Christian thought, however, is the association of the normal human desire and drive (along with the natural coupling of men and women in increasingly monogamous union) with the divine Love. Even in those Christian communions which refuse to list marriage as "one of the sacraments," there is still a sacramental quality or aspect in marriage. It is not regarded as merely a legalization of rape, for example, or an attempt to give social respectability and acceptance to sexual energies. On the contrary, it is in a profound way part of the divine purpose for the human race. Furthermore, the love of a man and a woman, finding its manifestation in their promised intention to live together faithfully for the whole of their mortal existence, in some manner reflects the kind of love which, for all Christians, is supreme and ultimate: it is the human participation in what one of the Anglican prayer books calls "the Love which is immortal" and "which is manifested to us in Christ Jesus our Lord."

The church has never claimed that it "married" people. What it says it does do, is witness their promises one to the other, for it is *they* (not the church) who are the "ministers" of the marriage. It does more, however. It pronounces, in the name of God in Christ, a blessing upon the union which the couple have agreed to enter. That blessing amounts to a declaration that here is a little colony of love, established in the midst of human life; and because it is such a colony, it is both accepted by the God who is Love and given by him the capability of enriching, strengthening, where need be correcting, each of the parties. Through that union in the usual course of events new life will be brought into the world; children will be born to the couple, children who are to be brought up in God's love and helped to realize, for themselves, the potentialities of human personality.

Marriage, thus conceived, is both a glorious and wonderful thing *and* a matter of enormous seriousness. That is why, again in familiar words from the marriage service, it is "not by any to be enterprised, nor taken in hand, unadvisedly, lightly, or wantonly," but "reverently, discreetly, advisedly, soberly, and in the fear of God." That last phrase, "the fear of God," might suggest to the ill-informed some state of fright, "being scared" of penalties that could be imposed by a terrible and overly-moralistic Judge. But its true meaning, as elsewhere the Prayer Book makes clear and as increasingly Christian thinkers are coming to see, is very different from that mistaken idea. "The fear of God" is the deepening sense that men have of the awe which they must feel in the presence of the "pure unbounded Love" which, in Dante's words, "moves the sun and the other stars." This is no fear awakened by terror; it is reverence in the presence of a Love that "will not let us go." To share one's life with another human being is to grasp something of the wonder of that Love as it is reflected in the imperfect yet dedicated love which we men can know one with another.

Chapter 6
The Homosexual Expression of Sexuality

In discussing the homosexual expression of human sexuality it will be necessary to follow a rather different line from that taken in the last chapter. This is because, even today, something of a "case" must first be made out for the man or woman who feels sexual attraction to his or her own sex and who desires some type of relationship with such an other. There is a suspicion, one might say a dislike, of homosexuality and homosexuals, even today when the fact of homosexuality and the presence among us of homosexuals are much more readily recognized and accepted.

Whether there has been an increasing number of homosexuals, male and female, in recent years, it is very difficult to say. But it *can* be said that they are much more a part of the social scene. Estimates as to their numbers vary, but it seems to be generally agreed that about 5 percent of the population should be included in this category—which would mean between two and three million men and women in the United Kingdom, about ten million in the United States, and in the world at large a quite enormous number of persons. Not all these are active homosexuals, as the phrase puts it; a considerable proportion very infrequently, if ever, express their sexual feelings in overt ways.

In many parts of the world the legal position of the homosexual has been much improved during recent years. This means, in practice, the homosexual male, since there have never been legal sanctions against the homosexual female. In England and Canada, for example, homosexual acts between consenting adults are no longer classed as criminal, while in many continental countries these are accepted without much question. Even in the United States, an oddly moralistic country despite its professed "freedom of action," the situation is considerably relaxed, although from time to time the police can make raids on homosexual bars and other such resorts or harass individual homosexuals. Novels have been written in almost every language portraying the homosexual and his life. Some distinguished leaders in various fields have confessed their homosexuality, too, without much damage to their reputation.

Furthermore the long-accepted stereotype of the homosexual seems to be disappearing. The idea that the homosexual male is an effeminate person with limp wrists and a high-pitched voice, usually rather "arty" in character, or that the homosexual woman is exaggeratedly masculine and loud and noisy: no longer do most people entertain such notions. Homosexuals are drawn from every section of the population. They may be bank directors or truck drivers, actresses or quite ordinary looking "home-bodies"; they may be well-educated and cultured or they may be uneducated and without cultural interests; they may be young boys in their teens or older men, young girls or matronly-looking women. In fact, anybody one meets *may* be a homosexual. In all their diversity of background, class, education, profession, social standing, there is but one thing which is common to them: their interest in their own sex and the direction of their sexual desire and drive to others of that sex.

Another significant fact in our time is that increasingly, as it seems to me, homosexuals are seeking for some kind of permanence in their relationship with one whom they can love. While promiscuity, the "one-night-stand," still continues, and while a great many (perhaps the majority) of homosexual men content themselves with these brief encounters, at the same time a growing minority want to find a relationship which will be on a more or less permanent basis. They want social acceptance of such a relationship too. It is certainly not easy for two men to "set up house" together, although women are able to do so with little difficulty. For men this is hard to do for several reasons, not least because of social disapproval or rejection. Yet granted the difficulties, more seem

60

to be attempting it; and one notices that quite young men are ready to show openly their love for another male, to travel with him, to share a flat, to live together. Often enough, there must be a surreptitious aspect to such relationships, but this seems to be decreasing.

In universities where a poll has been taken, the fact of homosexuality and of the possibility of homosexual unions, of greater or less permanence, appears to be taken for granted. There is little if any condemnation by the young; it is the older and more conventional who show disapproval, sometimes in unpleasant ways.

There can be no doubt that today those who discover themselves to be homosexual are much more likely to accept their particular sort of sexual drive, to attempt to find ways of satisfying it, and to demand (that is not too strong a word, in view of the several societies and other groups which have been formed in recent years) that they be regarded by the general public as entirely "normal" people, save for this one thing— which, in their view, is neither wicked nor criminal but something in which they have every right to rejoice. Most homosexuals do not wish to be "cured"; they do not consider their sexual interests a symptom of sickness. The psychologists who talk about homosexuality often generalize from the few men or women who consult them and who wish, for one reason or another, to be "changed"; but such men and women are not typical of the majority—they are indeed "sick"; perhaps, but so also are the heterosexuals who visit such psychologists. The ordinary homosexual, at least among those known to me, may find his life difficult, but he is glad to accept himself for what he is. What he wants is not to become a heterosexual but to find ways in which he can be as happy and fulfilled a homosexual as it is possible for him to be.

Finally, in concluding these preliminary remarks, we should notice that the homosexual tends to be a "sensitive" person. That adjective is not my own; it was first used in my hearing by a sympathetic practising psychiatrist, who told me that in his experience the notion that all homosexuals were "tough," inclined to "sadomasochism," etc., was quite mistaken. His conviction was that they were, for the most part, "sensitive" people, with keen aesthetic awareness and with a certain gentleness of character—hence, he said, the erroneous notion that they were "arty," since most people assume that only the "artistic" are thus sensitive.

What the homosexual most wants from life is the opportunity to be himself, to develop himself as a total personality. He wants to be a man, in the generic meaning of the word; that is, he wishes to move towards greater integration, to express himself and his possibilities, to be more

61

open in social contacts, to participate in society, to be responsible in his decisions. In this respect, then, the homosexual is not different from other people. The only difference is found in the particular type of sexual drive which is his. Of course to many this in itself will classify him as a "pervert," an entirely "abnormal" personality; but we have already argued that this is not the case, while in the sequel more will be said about the question. In any event, so far as his own feelings go, the homosexual is entirely "normal" and he sees no reason why he should not be accepted by his fellowmen and women as such.

If it be the case, as I believe, that men are personalities in the making, *men-on-the-way* in a processive world where things are "coming to be," our human condition is always "becoming"—we have not yet "arrived" at full manhood. The sexual desire and drive, so central to human beings, is integrated into that pattern of "becoming"—"Man never is/but wholly hopes to be," as Robert Browning put it—and plays its essential part in the on-going movement. For the heterosexual person, this is through relationships with somebody of the opposite sex; for the homosexual, it is and only can be through relationships with somebody of his own sex. To act responsibly, under control but without suppression, in sexual ways is one chief mode of human self-expression, with the homosexual as much as with the heterosexual.

It may be said, however, that while all this sounds right, the homosexual is not really a "nice person," since he wishes to act, in a physical fashion, in a way that is degraded. But is the homosexual physical relationship degraded? Often this view rests back on a distrust of the body, and would apply as much to the heterosexual as to the homosexual. Again, some would say that because the homosexual act cannot lead to the procreation of new life, it is wrong. But that no longer makes much sense to those who distinguish between sexuality as an expression of love and sexuality as the biological means for reproduction—even while at the same time they know that in heterosexual relations there is a close connection between the two. I believe that if sexuality is as central to man as I have urged, speaking as I have done in agreement with modern research as well as with what I take to be the deep intention in Jewish-Christian thought, then its expression through bodily activity is natural and right. The necessary means for the realization of human love is through *some* type of bodily activity, however much this may require control and however correct my earlier stress on "chastity" may have been. I am frank to say that I cannot see how the desire of the homosexual for bodily manifestation of his sexual drive is wrong, in and of itself;

62

nor can I see why, once this has been put under human controls, it is wrong for him to act upon it.

All this should not lead us to think that the homosexual confines his interest to the body of another. He responds, like everybody else, to the total personal impact of the other. What he desires is a personal relationship. In one of his novels, James Baldwin has put this very beautifully. In *Giovanni's Room* he shows David, the young American living in Paris, saying to Giovanni, his Italian lover, that he knows perfectly well *what* the latter wanted—obviously, sexual contacts of a physical sort. To which Giovanni replies, "You are the one who keeps talking about *what* I want. But *I* have been talking about *whom* I want." That puts my point very accurately and precisely. Granted that the homosexual male (if not the woman homosexual) is greatly interested in physical sex—granted, that is, that he is very largely "phallus-centred," as the document called *Towards a Quaker View of Sex* correctly says—it is the "who" rather than the "what" which is the heart of the matter for him. To be with another, to overcome loneliness through that companionship, to give himself and to receive from another: here is his deepest yearning. In this respect, surely, he is not so very different from his heterosexual brother.

The homosexual, like every other human being, wants to love and to be loved. His sexual drive is not simply a matter of physical desire; it is a matter of his whole personality. To be on the way to wholeness, he knows, requires that mutual love which has its physical grounding in his sexual nature but which is so much more than the purely physical. He asks that he be allowed by society to love and to be loved in the way that is possible and natural for him, whatever may be the case with other people. Once this is realized, everything else falls into place. The homosexual way of "making love," the interests which he has, the habits which are proper to him, can only be understood when they are set in this context. All contribute to and play their part in his movement towards becoming the man he would like to be. He requires deliverance from loneliness and isolation, which to him are so often a terrible reality; he wants a place where he can have the security which others find so readily. He needs liberation from the anxiety and the gnawing fear that because he is unaccepted his life is purposeless. He yearns for the "steadiness"—what the Latin calls *stabilitas*—which will enable him to face "the changes and chances of this mortal life." Perhaps above all his yearning is for freedom to be himself, as and for what he is, so that he *can* direct himself towards his proper fulfilment.

The Quaker report, to which we have referred, sees this clearly. That report centres its attention on the meaning of love, both human and divine; it recognizes the intimate relationship between the two. The document was prepared, we are told, by the need that was felt for a Christian attitude towards homosexuals; an enormous amount of work, including the hearing of evidence from many experts as well as discussion with admittedly homosexual men and women, was necessary before an agreed statement could be reached. The problems which the homosexual faces in contemporary society are stated frankly, but the report insists that "homosexual affection can be as selfless as heterosexual affection" and in consequence it concludes that "we cannot see that it is in some way morally worse." Furthermore, the report boldly affirms that "we see no reason why the physical nature of a sexual act should be the criterion by which the question of whether or not it is moral should be decided." It looks at the more personal side of homosexuality, too: "We are concerned with the homosexuals who say to each other, 'I love you,' in the hopeless and bitter awareness of a hostile criminal code and hypocritical public opinion"—the report appeared, of course, before the changes in the law following the Wolfenden Commission's recommendations in England.

The Quakers tell us, rightly, that "love cannot be confined to a pattern"; they affirm that "we need a release of love, warmth, and generosity into the world, in the everyday contacts of life, a positive force that will weaken our fear of one another and our tendencies towards aggression and power-seeking"; and they are ready to acknowledge that homosexual love is one of the ways in which this "love, warmth, and generosity" may be released. They warn against the evil present in all coercion and in attempts at seduction in homosexual as well as in heterosexual life. But their contribution is essentially positive and we may welcome the report as one of the first efforts to look at the homosexual condition, the homosexual situation, and the physical side of homosexual life with Christian concern and with truly human sympathy. They have even shown that the sordid aspects of homosexual life—the frequenting of public conveniences in an effort to find a sexual partner, the occasional "pick-up"; and the like—are very largely the result of society's so arranging things that only in such unhappy ways can the homosexual discover a means for the release of his sexual desires and some measure, inadequate and impermanent as such means must be, of companionship.

Christians are convinced that human fulfilment cannot be achieved by man alone. It does not matter so much whether we can *name* what it is, or who it is, which brings fulfilment; the deepest truth is that there is some hidden movement of love-in-action, working in the world and in human life to bring about realization of possibilities at each and every level of nature, history, and experience. The movement is thwarted by the recalcitrant egotism which is found in the world but it seeks to overcome this, not by coercive measures so much as by persuasive lures and attractions. This movement is interpreted by Christians as being the activity of the divine Lover whom we call God. In human existence that cosmic Lover uses, for his purpose of uniting and fulfilling, our little human loving; it is chiefly, although not only, in relationships with others that we can *become ourselves,* as we are intended to be, can be, should be. Certainly this interpretation is a matter of faith; it cannot be logically demonstrated, as if it were the conclusion of some philosophical syllogism.

Implicit in the experience of love, as humanly known, there is a religious dimension. It need not show itself in any explicitly religious language, but it is there. The homosexual knows this just as well as the heterosexual. I should wish to urge that in his loving, as in that of the heterosexual, there is participation in a cosmic Love which is more inclusive and more enriching than the particular human experience of love in this or that instance. In the movement towards fulfilment, towards becoming a person, there is the presence and the working of the active Love that is highest and deepest in the whole cosmic process.

Something of what I am urging is stated by James Baldwin in another of his novels. In *Another Country* Baldwin portrays two men who discover that they love one another. The two go to bed, innocently enough; by necessity they must share the same bed. They fall asleep; but during the night Vivaldo, one of the two men in the story, awakes to find that unconsciously he has "curled his legs, himself, around Eric." The other wakes too. Both are a little startled when they realize, in Baldwin's words, "that love had entered this bed." The story continues with a restrained yet certainly beautifully written description of what follows. I need not quote it here, but what takes place is a union of their bodies in various kinds of physical sexual activity. Then Baldwin describes what Vivaldo thought in respect to that activity: "He felt fantastically protected, liberated, by the knowledge that, no matter where, once the clawing day descended, he felt compelled to go, no matter what happened to him from now until he died, and even . . . if they should never lie in each other's arms again, there was a man in the world who loved him. All of his hope, which had grown so pale, flushed into life again. He loved Eric: it was a great revelation. But it was even more strange and made for an unprecedented steadiness and freedom, that Eric loved him."

The words which Baldwin uses in this narrative are worth attention:

"protected," "liberated," "steadiness," "freedom." They tell us what any and every man requires as he moves towards true fulfilment. The protection which comes from being accepted; the steadiness which gives him courage to live; the freedom to be himself in relationship with others; the liberation from anxiety and fear—here are some of the qualities which are required, if a human life is to move towards realizing its personal fulness. Without something of the sort, that life becomes inane and hopeless and there is no impelling drive to move it onwards. If homosexual love can provide these, it is a good thing; only the narrow-minded, the hyper-puritanical, the conventionally moral, would dare to deny its goodness.

Now the homosexual is likely to experience difficulty if he wishes to relate himself to a religious institution—that is, if he feels that he should not destroy his particular sexual urge but should remain, as he wants to remain, a homosexual. Admittedly his position is better today than in an earlier day. But there is always the fear of rejection. Yet often enough, what he needs more than anything else is the support which can be given in such participation in a religious community. Here there can be found so much that both appeals to him and offers him acceptance, from God through a human fellowship. An illustration is seen in an incident in still another novel about homosexual life, *Somewhere Between the Two* by the American writer James Little. In that novel a young man has discovered himself and found happiness in the love of another youth. Their love has included physical contacts from time to time. One day the young man, presumably a Roman Catholic, goes into a church and kneels before an altar upon which the sacrament is reserved. He prays with terrible earnestness for God's blessing upon the loving relationship which has meant so much to him; he prays that it may continue in all its wonder and beauty. And from this prayer he receives both comfort and strength.

I quite realize that some readers may feel a certain shock in the idea that homosexual love, with its physical contacts, may thus be brought into close association with the most sacred of all Christian beliefs—namely, the "real presence" of Jesus Christ in the sacramental elements of bread and wine. Would they feel the same sense of shock if a heterosexual, in prayer before the sacrament reserved, thought about and asked blessing on his love for his fiancée or his wife, with whatever physical acts might be associated with that love? I should suppose this very unlikely. Nowadays the average person would think that this was entirely proper and right, even if his ancestors in the Christian faith tended to think that it was not so. Yet, as the argument of this chapter has tried to show, there

66

is no sound reason, by human or Christian criteria, for making a sharp contrast between the love of that young man and the love of some other youth who has fallen in love with a girl.

This chapter has been very largely an attempt to put the case for the homosexual. In concluding it, we must return to our earlier insistence on the importance of responsibility, of control by love, and of utter respect for the other person in the relationship. The wrongness in homosexuality is to be found in exactly the same place as the wrongness in heterosexuality—that is, not in the condition, not in the accompanying desire for and practice of physical contact, but insofar as the homosexual, like the heterosexual, fails to be a responsible person, refuses to exercise control over his actions, and lacks real respect for the one whom he loves, or thinks he loves.

Granted that with such "safeguards," as we might put it, homosexual love can be as good an expression of sexuality as heterosexual love, there is no reason for the homosexual man or woman to feel ashamed of himself. There is every reason for him to accept himself—and there is every reason for society, including Christians and the Christian church, to accept him, too. What is required of him is that, being a homosexual, he shall be the *best* sort of homosexual possible. This will mean that he will try to find, as does the heterosexual, a partner with whom he can live in commitment or dedication, in giving-and-receiving, in mutuality, and in an enriching union. It will mean that tenderness, the strange combination of gentleness and strength, will characterize his relationship with the one he loves. He will not "flaunt" his sexual drive but he will not be afraid to act upon it, in the right circumstances and with the right person. He will seek to avoid, as will the heterosexual, promiscuous and chance contacts with persons whom he does not in fact love and with whom he can find only a momentary relief from sexual pressures. He will never coerce another into acts which to the other are unpleasant or which the other does not desire. And he will be alert to the dangers of seduction, whether of younger people or of others who may come to know him. In most ways, then, his sexual ethic will be like that of the ordinary heterosexual man or woman.

Doubtless to some readers, this entire chapter will seem mistaken; they will feel that an attempt to discuss a specifically *Christian* approach to the theology of human sexuality should not have included what to them will appear special pleading on behalf of the homosexual and homosexuality. It is because this feeling is undoubtedly present in many Christians that the discussion has been included—the intention has been, not

67

to make a "special case" for the homosexual, but to urge that he is *not* really "a special case" at all. More and more Christian theologians and writers on moral issues are coming to take this position—one need only cite Helmut Thielicke, Michael Keeling, Joseph Fletcher, and Kimball Jones, all of whom have lately published books which discuss the subject. The defect of *some,* not all, of these books is that they base their more sympathetic attitude on the notion that since all men are in sin, it ill behooves any one of us to look with disfavour upon any other. It is my own belief that this is far too negative a way of seeing the issue; hence in this chapter the effort has been to stress the positive aspects of homosexuality, the good which may be found in it, and the sense in which it may properly be seen as one of the possible ways for the expression of human sexuality, no more damaging (in any ultimate sense) to personality in the making than the more conventional and ordinary expressions of heterosexual love.

Sincerity, honesty, integrity: these are the qualities which one looks for in the sexual life of any human being. As it happens, these are what most homosexuals really want, too. When and if such a one comes to a priest, a minister, or a counsellor for help, he is not concerned to get rid of his particular sexual instincts; he is very much concerned to find help in achieving the sincerity, honesty, and integrity which he so much values. I believe that he *can* be helped and that this assistance will not expect that he must kill that capacity for love, in his own special way, which is for him the best thing he knows. Rather, to repeat what was said a few paragraphs earlier, he should be aided to become the best sort of homosexual possible for him to be. He should not be condemned for what he cannot help and for what, even if he could change it, he would not wish to alter—why should he? for this is his *only* way of loving and being loved. Since he is what he is, his need is to become the sort of man which he wants to be. And, as I have urged, that is really not too different from the sort of man any human being would wish to become.

Chapter 7
Frustrations and Distortions of Sexuality

Precisely because human love is so much the heart of human personality in the making and because central to that love is the sexual element in human existence, there is always the possibility of frustration and distortion. The reason for this is found in the capacity of man to make decisions for which he must of necessity assume responsibility. And because man is not an individual, separated from his brethren and able to live in splendid isolation, what any one man does is bound to affect others; when this influence has continued for long ages, with the wrong choices that this or that man has made having their infectious consequences in the lives of others, the situation is made very serious indeed. We have that state of affairs which classical theology has sought to describe by the use of the term "original sin."

Now in a processive world such as we know ours to be, much of the traditional theological picture can no longer be retained. It is useless as well as absurd to think that by a little tinkering here, a little refurbishing there, one can restore that picture to its pristine beauty and acceptability. On the other hand, because those who originally devised this theological picture were building on genuine facts of their experience, understood

69

in the light of their profound faith, there need be no doubt that in and behind what to us are the incredible outlines of the older theological scheme something very real and important was often being discerned. So it is with this matter of "original sin."

The way in which it has been presented, with the whole apparatus of man in a creation originally entirely good, with his historical act of decision and the "fall" that resulted, with the expulsion from the "Garden of Eden," and all the rest of it—this framework is no longer possible for us to accept. *But* the empirical fact, known to every man in the depths of his experience and through his serious reflection, the fact which that ancient tale sought to assert and explain, is plain enough. Man *is* in frustration and *is* distorted; he *is* twisted in his loving and hence in his living. Anybody who fails to see this only convicts himself of superficiality.

Perhaps we could put the situation in this way: Man is created in the image of God, intended to live in love, in self-giving mutuality with others in the context of a life integrated into a pattern through relationship with his loving Creator. Thus he is made to become a personality, making the decisions which will bring him to fulfilment. This is his God-intended goal; this is the meaning of his existence; the realization or making actual of this is his deepest and most enduring joy. But as a matter of fact, he deflects and distorts this pattern, by his own choices made in responsible freedom; the consequence is damage both to individuals and to the society of which they are part. Furthermore, since the desiring and willing of every man is affected by the general situation in which he finds himself, he continues to make wrong decisions. His "wills and affections," as the ancient prayer tells us, must be seen for what they are: "unruly," disordered, and without the full control which alone can make their proper exercise a possibility.

Nowadays we have no need to apologize for this kind of description of man and his condition. There was a period, ending with World War II, when an optimistic perfectionism was the popular mood. Talk about sin, whether "original" or "actual," was regarded as the obsession of a few out-dated religiously-minded people. But we have been forced by the events of our time to see more deeply. The account of "the fall of man" in the early chapters of Genesis is not scientifically accurate history; but what that story is telling us is the truth—the story speaks to each of us and to our human condition. It is existentially apt. Man *is* in fact both frustrated and distorted, so that he is not able "of himself to help himself." Not only Christians but thinkers and writers of very different persuasion agree about this.

On the other hand, the reaction from silly optimism should not lead us to the opposite extreme. There are some Christian theologians, just as there are some interpreters of the "secular" scene, who are guilty of exactly such an extreme reaction. They tell us that man is so depraved, so much a creature of sin, that his situation is at worst entirely hopeless and that at best he can only be rescued from his wickedness by an intrusive act of God from outside. But in our processive universe this picture of "intrusion" no longer makes sense. *Help* man does need, if he is to be recovered from his sad state; but that help is not by some in-thrust from outside the world—rather, it is by the utilization, by man himself but more significantly by the activity of the ever-present and ever-operative Love which works within the whole cosmos, of the energies and drives which are in the creation. In other words, it is by the proper lure of the potentialities which are not so much inserted into the process from some remote source called "God," as ingredient in any and every occasion for decision through the mysterious but real patterning or ordering which cosmic Love makes possible.

In his present condition, man seeks for self-gratification in ways that are not conducive to his best good. He is impatient of long-range goals and of the necessary control of his desires by the highest possible good—the good that is nothing other than the divine Love. He finds it not only difficult, but impossible, continually to order his life so that the enduring goods are always sought and the lesser goods put in their subordinate place. In other words, he fails in the making of his person, in community with his fellows and in and under God. Yet God remains the supreme good, dwelling in and working through all lesser goods; and so men are always, and inescapably, seeking for him, even when they seek him in the wrong ways. They seek him, so to say, by indirection. This is the explanation of the dis-ease (notice that we have written *dis-ease,* inquietude) which is so marked a characteristic of every man who is not willing to let himself sink to the merely animal level; and even when he does let himself do this, he cannot remain there, since somehow the lure of a better gets possession of him and moves him to efforts which, however unsuccessful, are towards a glimpsed good. Man discerns that the lesser goods are not adequate, even when he feels impelled to go after them.

It is the affirmation of the Christian gospel that this situation, however serious and tragic, is not irremediable. Through the forces for good latent in the creation, through the continuing pressures of Love through the creation—not occasionally intrusive but consistently operative—a possibility is offered to human existence. That possibility is response to Love, with a reordering or repatterning which will enable right choices to be made. Fulfilment is offered, so that personality may be made actual in the fashion which God intends and which men may recognize as being indeed their proper goal. Everywhere and always this process of renewal and enablement is at work. The Christian claims that in Jesus Christ this process is visibly and decisively enacted, so that in him we have the classical instance, hence the vivifying power, of God's way and will for men. But to discuss this further would bring us into the area which theology calls "soteriology" or the doctrine of "salvation"; that important subject is not, however, the subject of this book.

Man is a sexual being who seeks and requires fulfilment in union with others of his race; specifically, with *an* other, with whom he can be in the closest and deepest relationship of love. That is the means by which he is enabled, proximately, to move towards fulfilment in the Other who moves in and through all others—in God himself. But since this is so, there can be no area of human experience in which human frustration and distortion expresses itself so readily as in sexual life.

But this must not be misunderstood. Sin and sex are not identical. To have assumed that they were was the great mistake of many thinkers who wrongly believed that they were stating "Christian" principles. We have made sufficiently clear in the earlier part of this book that the physical act of sexual relations is not an evil; we have also urged that the way of sexual expression known as homosexual cannot in itself be regarded as distorted or wrong. Sexuality is good; it can never be evil in itself. But it *can* be distorted, as it is frustrated, so that in its functioning (to use an inadequate word) it becomes instrumentally evil. What *is* sinful is man's arrogance, his seeking to possess and use others, his over-weening self-assertion against the right ordering of things—in a word, his pride when it leads him to act as if he, and he alone, controls the world and can do with it as he wishes.

Thus man can and does use this particular instrumentality of sexual existence in such a fashion that he distorts and disarranges the divinely-intended pattern of things. When man's sexual life is thus distorted, we witness both a symptom and a reacting cause of human wrong-doing. Not always is this crude and blatant; it can be very subtle and hence all the more difficult to discern. The use of another personality for one's own ends is utter disregard of the good of the other; it is evil, even if not so obviously evil, as the actual raping, physically, of the other's body. Soames Forsyte in John Galsworthy's *Forsyte Saga* is "a man of prop-

72

erty" who considers his wife a possession for his own enjoyment as he desires. It is only when he comes to see that the consequences of such misuse are disastrous for himself that he recognizes the situation for what it is; and then it is too late to do anything for himself, while at the same time he can see that he has infected a succeeding generation with the virus of his own possessive and disproportionate sexuality.

In the vulgarity of much that is today written and said about sex, we see another illustration of the same principle. The sexual consciousness is reduced to its lowest terms, with no penumbra of meaning in terms of true love, with no representation of self-giving, tenderness, commitment, the willingness to receive. Then we see only sheer ugliness. *Corruptio optimi pessima*—the best, when it is corrupted, becomes the worst.

In order to bring sexuality into its rightful place, as the expression of man's drive to love and to be loved, it must be under control. The control proper to love is control by love and in love. The dissipation of man's life by entirely uncontrolled assertion of immediate desire produces deterioration, halts the making of personality, and tends to the destruction of community. We shall say more about control later in this chapter. Here we stress that proximate attainment of human fulfilment, with release from the bondage of selfishness (in its worst sense), is found when a man or woman "loses himself" in love for another of his own kind. Possibly that is why the word "helpmate" has been applied to the other partner in marriage, for the other here can aid towards release. That too is why the love of man for man, woman for woman, can release energies which renovate and invigorate the personality. Ultimately, all these human loves are channels for the divine Lover, who is the final source of all loving. Thus sexual union has been taken, in Christian thought, as the analogue, the sacramental symbol, of the union of the creature with the Creator. For it can be said in all reverence that God yearns that his creatures shall respond to him and does all that can be done to make that response possible. All of our human loving, no matter how distorted, is a reflection of the eternal reality of God *as* Love. When directed aright, when properly ordered, it becomes what in principle and intention it has always been: a participation in the divine Love, made visible and available in this world of space and time.

John Macmurray has defined chastity as "emotional sincerity." Surely he is right in doing so. Traditionally, chastity has meant complete abstention from sexual relationships; but as we have already seen, this is a narrowing of the term. It is a far too negative interpretation and it makes nonsense of the goodness of sexuality. It suggests, for example,

73

that a married couple, deeply devoted to one another, are much "better" when they never engage in sexual contacts. What is required of man, if he is to make his personality in this world of "becoming," is an honest, open, glad, acceptance of sex, and its equally honest, open, and glad expression in action. The sexual drive, employed for the deepening of love and hence for the enrichment of the personal existence of those who act on it, is *real* chastity. It is genuine "emotional sincerity"; and it is as much possible for a homosexual as for a heterosexual human being.

To say that chastity is "emotional sincerity" is also to say that it is love in operation—love acting as love must act when it is truly love, with an intentionality as nearly complete as finite "personalities in the making" can show. True love is "honest and above-board"; nothing is hidden, nothing held back. It is the outreach of one to the other, including recognition in heart and mind and expression in act, of the truth that each is a growing personality, not a thing to be used for immediate self-satisfaction.

If that is the case, men and women who engage in the sexual act can be entirely chaste, while a married couple who are not thus honest with themselves and with each other, or who are guilty of coercion or pressure exercised upon the other, are not chaste. The same principle holds true for the homosexual; if he is not honest with himself and the other, if he tries to exercise pressure on the other, he is an unchaste person. It is not the nature of his partner, the fact that he is of the same sex, which is responsible for the unchastity; it is the quality of the relationship. Possessive, self-assertive, coercive sexuality is what is wrong and sinful— that is, distorted and twisted.

The tendency towards masochism, in which one delights in hurting oneself either physically or psychologically; the similar tendency towards sadism, in which one delights in hurting another . . . here are the worst manifestations of the possible distortion of human sexuality. Tenderness, true sharing, mutuality, is lacking in contacts of those sorts. As we have been learning from psychological analysis, the deep roots of those tendencies are found in the factors which have inhibited or damaged the capacity to love. This is why at every stage of human life, from early childhood on, the only sound and healthy situation is when love is shown to others. A child who has not known love is likely to become an adult who cannot love. The human condition, thanks to the long history of lovelessness, in greater or less degree, makes the giving and receiving of love a matter of influence, training, surroundings, environmental factors, which can in some fashion modify the inheritance of the race in its love-

74

less aspect. Yet that inheritance is not entirely loveless; it is *mixed*—hence what needs stressing from the earliest days of childhood is the positive side, the loving aspect; what needs control is the loveless side, the possessive, coercive, self-assertive aspect.

So far we have spoken largely of the distortions of sexuality. There are also the frustrations. To a very large extent these are beyond control. There are many pressures which inhibit men and women from loving as they wish; there are many influences that interfere seriously with the love that is deep within them. To a certain degree these are simply *given:* we live at a certain time, in a certain place, under certain conditions. There is very little we can do about these. The limitations they impose are limitations upon the area of our free human decisions; they are also limitations upon the amount of responsibility which we may assume for the decisions which we do make. Hence they are not within the control of the personal agent. And in consequence, choices made within those limitations cannot be regarded as in and of themselves evil choices. At the same time, the situation itself, insofar as it is to whatever extent remediable, is an unsatisfactory one—in religious language, it is "displeasing to God"; therefore it is also objectively a false situation, an evil one, even a "sinful" one. Where personal responsibility enters is in what this or that man or woman *does* with his frustrations. He may permit them to embitter him; he may allow them to drive him to an introverted concern for himself; he may try to break out in ways which are damaging to himself and to others. *Then* the frustrations become the occasion for distortion. Certainly each of us must judge charitably, so far as others are concerned; but for ourselves, we should not be too self-indulgent. We *could* have acted otherwise. We *might* have refused to allow these limitations to drive us into unloving activity. If we did not, then we *are* responsible for what we have made of ourselves, even when the circumstances were appallingly bad and the frustrations almost unbearable.

There are one or two matters which often come up for discussion when the *wrong* side of sexual expression is considered. For example, what about the securing of sexual satisfaction by auto-erotic means? Is masturbation "a sin"? If so, when and how? That is one subject which requires attention, although nothing like so much attention as some moral theologians have given it.

For the very young person, especially boys, masturbation seems a very natural and inevitable practice. It used to be condemned as the most grievous of sins; nowadays, thanks to better knowledge, it is not so regarded. Nor should it be regarded in that way when it is found among

75

older persons, male or female. The question is one of context, rather than about the act itself. If auto-erotic practices become a *substitute* for whatever other-regarding sexuality is possible for a given person, it is so much a lesser good that it can be seen as wrong. Normally, the young person grows up to desire to express his sexuality with another, whether this be the more usual one of heterosexuality or the less usual (but, as I have argued, not therefore wicked) one of homosexuality. The adult who is unable thus to grow is a pathetic spectacle, surely; we need not indulge in harsh judgement about him, but we can still think that his situation is tragic. In any event, masturbatory practices are wrong only in context; they may be right, even desirable, when *all* possible relationships with others are cut off and the only opportunity for relief of strong irresistible sexual drives is through self-stimulation. Cases differ, as do situations. But what is now known to be a fact is that nobody can ruin his physical health by masturbation; it is the anxiety and fear and guilt which well-meaning but misguided persons or books have awakened that causes the disturbance, both mental and bodily, often associated with masturbation.

Another question concerns the use by married couples of contraceptive means to control the number and spacing of children. Enough has already been said to indicate only a very erroneous view of the meaning of sexuality in marriage could deny the rightness of such preventive measures —although a couple who for selfish reasons refuse to themselves the birth of any children are most certainly *not* choosing the best way in love. The number and spacing of children is one thing; the absolute refusal to let love, under any circumstances, lead to procreation is another. The two are often confused, not only by ordinary people but also (alas!) by those who write about moral issues, not least within Christian circles.

We have already spoken of pre-marital and extra-marital sexuality, as well as about homosexual relationships. It remains only to say something about the more positive side of human sexuality; we must conclude with *that,* lest the picture be far too emphatic about frustrations and distortions. Indeed, one of the sad aspects of much that has traditionally been written about sex is that the darker side has been stressed and the impression given that Christians regard the whole subject with grave suspicion. Sometimes the impression is even more unfortunate, for it can be made to seem that Christians could wish that man were not a sexual being at all—they would have preferred disembodied, purely spiritual existence. But as we have argued, such a position is both absurd and unchristian.

So let us say with all possible emphasis that human sexuality is a very

76

good thing. It is part of man's nature, very central to his personality in the making. It is part of God's creation, a creation which the myth in Genesis tells us God found to be "very good." It is tied in with and expressive of the urgent desire to love, which is deepest and highest in the universe. Hence it is intimately related to God himself, who in Christian faith is himself nothing other than sheer love-in-action: "his nature and his name is Love," says one of Wesley's hymns. Those who denigrate sexuality are unconsciously blaspheming against God himself.

In our own age, which has reacted so strongly against the negative and repressive attitude towards sexuality which marked the Victorian mentality—or what we *call* that mentality, for perhaps the Victorians were not quite so inhuman as we have been told they were—there is an urgent desire to express sexuality in a free way. Critics of the age talk about the "permissive society," which they regard as a shocking and dangerous relaxation of standards. But this suggests that they are often unwilling to face the facts. There is much more "permissiveness," to be sure; yet this may well be seen as amounting to honesty, rather than to a rejection of all standards. Many of us feel that the younger generation is much more honest, both in its attitude to sexuality and in its expression of it, than an earlier generation. At least, members of today's younger generation do not pretend to be other than they are—that pretending, maybe, was the *real* mistake of the much-decried Victorians. Another name for it would be hypocrisy. Most young men and women today are not hypocritical, whatever other faults they may have.

These young people accept their sexuality, not grudgingly but gladly. They see that the real "obscenity" in human life is not in sexual desires and acts but in hatred, injustice, lack of understanding of others—and they are right in this. They are not obsessed with human sexuality, although some of their critics claim that they are. But it is the critics who are obsessed by it; their obsession is the result of a repression of something deeply and genuinely human, to a very large degree a repression born of fear of something they do not know how to handle. My own belief is that a world which is modelled more after the patterns of the younger generation's yearnings may not be a nicely settled and conventional world but it will be a world where honesty is more prevalent, where decent human relations are more frequently found, and where life is more happily and more beautifully lived. The job of older persons is not to spend time condemning the supposed excesses of younger ones; rather, it is to bring to bear on sexual questions the wisdom but not the prejudices of the past ages. And that can be done without adopting an attitude of *de haut en bas* and without assuming that "new occasions" do *not* make much of our understanding of "ancient good" irrelevant and meaningless.

We are greatly in need of a new moral code, so far as sexual behaviour is concerned. The older one simply does not work any more. There is no use in spending one's time regretting the fact and criticizing those who are either unable or unwilling to live by it. The new code should be positive, not negative; it should stress the goodness of sex, not its possible evils and dangers—those will soon enough be realized. The code, if that is the right word to apply to it, will find its centre in the reality of human loving; it will be built upon an appraisal of human personality which recognizes its processive character; and it will be prepared to make allowances for human imperfection, precisely because it will know that man is not a finished product but is very much "in the making." It will see human sexuality in its total context, not as a restricted area of life which may be rejected at will. I believe that such an approach will produce an ethic that is both workable *and* Christian. It is a tragedy that so many of those who are best equipped to assist in the development of such an ethic are prepared to miss the opportunity offered them today, and to devote so large a portion of their time and effort to denunciation and attack. They are doing a great deal of harm, not only to those whom they might well have helped, but also to the possibility of making a soundly Christian understanding of human sexuality available to others. We may be grateful that some Christian thinkers, risking their own reputation and daring to speak boldly and positively, have been working in the right direction. May their tribe increase!

Chapter 8
An Ethic of Sexuality

The last chapter ended with a plea for the development of a new pattern in respect to sexual life—a pattern which will be humane and truly human, possible to accept and follow, and in its spirit and intention thoroughly Christian. In this chapter we shall try to indicate some of the ingredients in such an ethic. The suggestions will necessarily be tentative and it is not our intention to propose a detailed and complete "code"— indeed, should we attempt such a code, the main argument of this book would be denied. For if by a code we mean a set of commandments, handed down to be obeyed, then it is precisely such a thing which has brought us to our present confused situation.

There *has been* a code of that sort. Often enough it was called the "Christian ethic" of sex; as a matter of fact, a good deal of it was simply a canonization of the conventions which developed in the nineteenth century, to a considerable degree the reflection of a so-called "Victorian" morality but miscalled when that description was applied. What was thought to be "Victorian" was in England largely a non-conformist (in the sense of a middle-class mercantile type which was identified more or less correctly with the moralism then often found in the "independent," Wesleyan, Baptist, and other denominations) ethic or morality. In the

United States the same development took place, although in that land it was due to the continuing influence of a negative puritanism, very different from the position of the actual Puritans who settled New England during the seventeenth century.

In that conventional ethic, there were Christian elements, of course. By a certain reading of the Bible, oddly enough with an emphasis on the Old Testament, but with a narrowness that the continuing Jewish tradition seems to have avoided, it was possible to work out a repressive attitude towards sexuality. And when that was combined with the long-established strain of docetic thought which has continually dogged the more central Christian tradition of acceptance of man's bodily nature, the result was what one might have expected: the "sexual ethic" against which so many modern men and women, above all younger people, are in revolt.

This pattern was essentially negative in spirit. It was a bourgeois morality, rooted in the bourgeois mentality so dominant in English-speaking lands. It distrusted the flesh, looked with suspicion on anything sexual which had not been given sanction through the legal institution of marriage, and tended even then to be evaded by many who outwardly supported it: hypocrisy was very prevalent in many quarters of society. Two illustrations of such hypocrisy may be cited. A very distinguished churchman, honoured by his contemporaries as a great leader, was married and had children. So far so good. But it has lately been discovered, thanks to the finding of a collection of his letters, that he also maintained a second household, with a mistress by whom he had other and unacknowledged children. So shocking was this discovery that the scholar who by chance came upon the letters and through enquiry traced the details of the "second woman" and her children, determined that for the present at least it was wiser not to include any reference to the matter in a biography of this famous man. All that was only a few years ago; the life of the churchman was lived from about 1840 until the early part of this century.

The other illustration is the now fairly-well established fact that during the latter part of the nineteenth century there were more prostitutes, used by distinguished public leaders who in the eye of the people were supposed to be ardent defenders of "purity" in sexual affairs, than anyone had thought likely. London was filled with them, and so was New York. Well-furnished brothels, with inmates prepared to give satisfaction to a wide variety of sexual tastes, were part of the scene in the great cities. They provided amusement for the rich and powerful; and it was precisely

80

those men who were generally taken to be the stalwart supporters of the conventional sexual code.

But altogether apart from this hypocrisy, the code itself was a very odd thing. It assumed that women had no sexual desires or, if they had them, they should never express them. "Nice women" disliked sex and only "submitted" to it because it was their wifely duty. Men might be allowed to "sow their wild oats" when young, but always secretly and with women who were not socially accepted; when they came to the age of responsible maturity and were obliged to assume positions of importance they were no longer to engage in such escapades but were to "settle down," as the saying went. Homosexuality, of course, was never mentioned, although we have no reason to think that there were many fewer men or women of that type than in later times. It was possible for such persons to find companions, but the whole matter was hushed up, the companions usually were of an undesirable sort, and when by accident it became known that so-and-so did engage in such contacts there was a public scandal.

It is hardly necessary to mention the extraordinary teaching which was commonly given about auto-erotic practices. Boys were told that if they indulged in masturbation they would go crazy or damage their physical health. Odd devices were invented and sold to make it impossible to engage in self-stimulation. The harm done to young people was enormous, creating a sense of guilt which was often very serious and might lead to the mental disturbance or physical upset which the practice itself never produces but which fear and guilt can create in any young person. And relationships between boys and girls were supposed to be entirely without physical contacts, to avoid any possibility of these contacts the institution of the chaperone was used.

Somebody has said that the sexual ethic which we have inherited was marked by fear of conception, infection, or detection: the possibility of the birth of bastard offspring, the possibility of venereal disease, or the possibility of being "found out" as one who was heterosexually or homosexually promiscuous. Of course the code was not phrased in such negative terms; it was worded in such a way that it might be made to appear as a call to purity, chastity, monogamy, decency. But as a matter of fact, the code in practice was almost entirely negative in its approach, negative in its attitude to sexuality, and negative in its distrust of any bodily experience which the conventions of the day did not accept. It was not so sinful to make money by subtly dishonest commercial practice, by hidden cheating, or by manipulation of the "market"; it was highly sinful to express one's sexual desires in any way save through marriage—and even then, it was thought better to restrain one's sexuality so far as possible.

Now I realize that in what has been written in the last few paragraphs I have exaggerated. The picture was not so black as I have painted it. There were some who took a different and healthier line, although they were disliked and often persecuted. But in general I believe that what has been written is near enough to the truth; and in any event it is an accurate portrayal of how the matter seemed to many people. Furthermore, it is how the matter seems now to young people who look back at that hundred years or so with disgust and horror. How could a code so inhumane, so lacking in understanding, so negative, have been accepted by so many for so long? That is the question younger folk have asked. And their own attitude, as well as much in contemporary sexual behaviour, is largely a reaction to what they have reason to believe was taught and enforced during the not too distant past.

So much by way of comment on the sexual ethical pattern which most of our contemporaries have simply rejected. What is to take its place? For nearly a quarter of a century, *nothing* has taken its place. By this I mean that there has been a sort of ethical chaos, so far as sexual expression is concerned. Some have tried to revive the older principles, but their efforts have been almost entirely unsuccessful. Others have advocated a position in which *no* principles of any sort should be attempted. Most have simply drifted, doing what they pleased as and when they pleased, yet feeling unhappy about a sexual life which had no guide-lines of any sort.

The interesting and important thing in quite recent years has been the emergence of a set of principles, as we might call them, which have come into existence largely through the experience and reflection of younger people. They have had little help from those who were supposed to be in a position of leadership, religious or moral—such people have generally stood for what they thought were traditional Christian standards but were (as I have argued) largely conventions derived from nineteenth-century patterns. In consequence, younger men and women have been obliged to think for themselves. It is astonishing that so much of their thinking has led to conclusions which are basically Christian as well as profoundly humane.

My own first introduction to this newer and younger attitude came from conversations with undergraduates of most varied background, in some of the great universities of Britain and North America. What I heard from them was confirmed by investigation into the thinking of young people from other levels of society and from a reading of surveys and "opinion polls" contained in studies by sociologists and psychologists. And I should sum up what I have learned by saying that the great majority of young people would say that the key to all sexual behaviour is found in what one young man said to me: "What we believe about sexual conduct is that it must be characterized by permissiveness, with affection, and in full acceptance of responsibility." There are three words here, each of which requires consideration: permissiveness, affection, and responsibility. To that consideration we now turn.

It is easy enough to denounce "permissiveness" as the equivalent of license. But that is not the sense in which the word is intended, either here in our discussion or by the young people with whom one talks on the subject. By "permissiveness" we mean a recognition of the fact that every human being, by virtue of his being human, must be given the "permission" to make his own decisions. He is a free agent; part of his humanity, his personality in the making, is his capacity and his right to "decide for himself," as we say. Otherwise he is being treated as a puppet, a pawn on a chessboard, something which can be ordered or moved about with no regard for his own rights as a man. Certainly permissiveness in *that* sense is integral to the existence of any society which is not totalitarian. One of the complaints that citizens of democratic societies make of Russia, for example, is that this kind of permissiveness does not seem to exist there; so also in Nazi Germany.

Rules cannot be imposed on other people, unless those rules are such that they win free assent. This does not imply that there are no limits to what may be "permitted"—that limit is reached when one's actions deny to others *their* right to free decision, or when some course of action is obviously and patently damaging to the life of the community as a whole. To work out the precise point at which such a limit is reached requires all the political ingenuity of the men whom we have elected to be our leaders. But surely the point is not to be found in respect to the expression of sexual life, as the ordinary person experiences it. Orgies which involve a great many people may very well be socially deleterious; I should think that they are. But what two people do in private, by mutual consent, is nobody's business but their own. This applies as much to homosexual contacts as to heterosexual and recently the law in England has recognized the fact.

Nor does the insistence on "permissiveness" mean that "anything goes." The two other words which have been quoted from an undergraduate make this clear. But "permissiveness" *does* mean that society, through its police or its law-making agencies, is in no position to dictate to anybody what he shall do; this he must decide for himself, within the commonly-agreed social limits (whatever they are) which preserve public order and common decency. To give but one example, and that a fairly obvious one: the man who indulges in what we call "indecent exposure" is a public nuisance and an offense to his neighbours. "Permissiveness" must not be interpreted to mean that he shall be allowed, or "permitted," to engage in such exposure how and when he will. But if in the privacy of his home, or in the presence of friends who enjoy this sort of thing, he walks about naked, it is nobody's business, certainly not the law's, to put him in gaol. The same principle applies in many other connections. The establishment of the limits is both difficult and necessary, but the principle of free decision must be allowed up to those limits.

My young friend also used, it will be remembered, the word "affection." If no morality can be enforced or imposed, since to do this removes it altogether from the realm of morality and puts it in the category of legal enactment or dictatorial control in which the *moral agent* vanishes, any pattern of behaviour must be based upon understanding and participation with others. *They* must be considered. So there is a very general sense in which "affection" can be taken to mean simply fellow-feeling and proper consideration of other people. But in the specifically sexual realm, the term means *love*. If it suggests only a kindly attitude or a "liking" which is but for the moment, it is not affection in the deepest and truest sense of the word. My young friend meant exactly what in this book we have been discussing under the word "love." And that introduces another and very important factor into the moral pattern in respect to sexual expression.

Do I, or do I not, genuinely love this or that person? Of course we are not able to say, with absolute certainty, that what I feel for another is love in the ultimate sense. But then, as we have urged, the real question is whether or not we are moving towards such a relationship, not whether we have arrived finally at the goal. I must ask myself whether I wish to commit myself totally, body and soul, to that other; whether I feel about the other the willingness to receive as well as the readiness to give; whether there is the possibility of some genuine mutuality between us; whether I am expectant of the other's development in the course of our relationship; whether a communion or association between us will be realizable and for the best growth of each of us towards that fulfillment of potentiality which is the "subjective aim" of every human life. There is

84

no chance for logical certainty here; I cannot *prove* love. What I can do, if the signs point positively to love, is to make the venture, take the risk.

Here, as we have seen, there is no place for coercion or pressure. Love is not expressed when I force somebody to do something I want. Love acts by persuasion, by lure, by invitation, depending always on the other's response to that persuasion, lure, invitation. And the response, to be genuine, cannot be other than the free decision of the person whom one loves. So much ought to be clear. It is only a different way of insisting that not only I myself, but my partner or friend or lover, must also be permitted free decision as an integral element in his human existence as a personality being made through his own choices.

Then there was the third word, "responsibility." Now that word has two meanings: on the one hand, the *response* which we make to somebody else; on the other hand, our *acceptance of the consequences* entailed in that response, taken as being really our own and not to be fobbed off onto somebody else.

The late Richard Niebuhr, shortly before his death, finished a book called *The Responsible Self*. In it he argued that one of the distinctive elements in human existence, and the clue to man's moral life, is found precisely in this concept of personally-accepted responsibility for what one does. Such responsibility rests ultimately upon the capacity of man freely to respond; nobody can be held "responsible" for an action that has been forced upon him against his will. Here "responsibility" and the "permission" to decide freely are seen in their close relationship; in a way, they are two sides of the same coin. It is this acceptance of responsibility, with due attention to consequences not only for myself and another but for the whole social milieu, which makes utterly impossible completely "thoughtless" behaviour. No person is truly responsible unless he considers what is entailed in this or that action for which he freely decides. To that degree at least each of us is a rational being; we are able to think about the results of our actions. Doubtless we do not have complete awareness of those results; doubtless there are indirect and unexpected consequences of any action. But so far as we are able, we must think about what we do.

This is not saying that there can be no spontaneity in human action. On the contrary, it is saying that through long training, through consideration of past experiences, through recognition of other people's ideas and attitudes, and through a vast amount of other data, we find ourselves "formed" in such a way that we can act responsibly in this or that given situation without having to spend hours of preliminary theorizing. In at least one tradition of Western thought, conscience has been defined as "the mind of man considering his proper decisions and actions." But conscience is made into what it is by our past choices, our surrounding environment, our open-ness to possibilities, and the like. The truly "conscientious"—that is, the really "responsible"—man need not worry about every slightest decision; he will have exercised himself sufficiently to be able spontaneously to act—yet to act "responsibly." He will make mistakes from time to time. Nobody thinks he is infallible save the moral prig, and *his* assumed infallibility is a sign of his inhumanity and often also of his inability to recognize human limitations.

Now let us apply these three terms to the sexual expression of human personality. In my sexual life, I must make my own responsible decision about what I shall or shall not do. I must make this decision with full regard for other people and above all for the one whom I love. I must never coerce or force another into situations where the other's right to equally free decision is denied. In everything that is done I must take full responsibility, recognizing that there are always consequences with which I must deal—and I dare not say that those consequences are only to be assumed by the other person or by other people.

It is my conviction that these three words, given the significance that has been argued in our discussion, provide us with a very good starting place for any viable sexual ethic. But of course we cannot stop just there. More must be said or we shall have left the matter at the purely "formal" stage. How do we give "content" to what has been said?

First of all, by relating what has just been said about permissiveness, affection, and responsibility to our earlier attempt to sketch what it means to be a man. We need to set those three key words in the context of personality in the making. We must bear in mind the capacity of man to move through decision to realization of possibility, his ability to communicate with others through words but more profoundly by "being with" those others, his dynamic thrust forward towards union with others in the common life, above all his yearning to love and to be loved. With this we need also to remember that for a Christian the lure which draws men to fulfilment of potentiality is ultimately the divine Lover who provides each entity in the creation with its "initial aim" for realization, surrounds each entity with invitations towards increasing good, and through the instrumentality of created things offers a relationship with himself that provides the *summum bonum* or highest good available to man.

We must also see how the three key words are related to those characteristics of love to which we drew attention: the commitment of self, the

86

open-ness to the other in giving of self and readiness to receive the other's gift of self, the hopefulness, the mutuality leading to union one with the other—and in and through these, tenderness, in which gentleness is combined with strength. Finally, we need to see how the frustrations which circumstances impose upon man's loving, above all the ever-present possibility of decisions which are damaging to human integrity and self-respect, and the accumulated mass of past and present wrongness in human relationships, can have their tragic affect upon the way in which each of us responds to others.

All of this is to be borne in mind, while at the same time we need to stress particularly the *embodiedness* of man—his physical nature, the bodily means of self-expression, the way in which sexuality is a matter both of sense and of spirit. None of these factors can be forgotten, although they need not be vividly in the forefront of our thinking every moment. What they amount to is that man is made to love and to be loved, that this making is still going on, that it needs to be seen in terms of responsible action, that the free man is the one who makes his own decisions (within the limits possible to him) and exercises the proper controls, and that there are frustrations and distortions of which he must be aware and against which (so far as his own choices are concerned) he must guard himself. All this, as well, in the context of life-in-community, the necessary existence of each of us with other human beings who like us are personalities in the making.

So it may be concluded that a viable sexual ethic will have the following essential ingredients:

1. Whatever one does, in terms of sexual manifestation, is to be an expression of love, rather than an effort to satisfy the merely animal lusts. Yet we must not forget that those "animal" desires are part of the total human structure, in themselves good, but needing right control lest they get "out of hand."

2. In all sexual activity, coercion and pressure can have no place, for they are a denial of love. This rules out seduction of the unwilling and any form of "rape."

3. Cruelty, whether subtle or vicious, is the denial of love and cannot be permitted. Sadism and masochism are the extreme cases of such cruelty, inflicted either upon others or inflicted (or desired) on oneself: in whatever form these show themselves, they are inhuman.

4. Nobody should be urged into kinds of sexual activity that are offensive to him or seem wrong in his own eyes. Whatever sexual practices are adopted, they must be pleasing to both parties involved.

5. In any and every sexual activity, those who engage in it must accept the responsibility for whatever it entails, whether this is the emotional state of the other person, a child who may result from that contact, or anything else. We cannot contract out of this responsibility without showing ourselves callous, indifferent, hence inhuman and unloving. To attempt to contract out is to deny our responsible manhood and to cut off the possibility of growth.

6. For most people, most of the time, in most places, the usual way of finding sexual satisfaction will be through a commitment in married life. That commitment will arise from love one for the other; the sexual activity, in the physical sense, will then be an expression and a strengthening of the love they share. There will be some (in actual figures, a considerable number) whose only way of sexual expression is homosexual, with another person of their own sex. In their case, the aim should be at establishing a relationship with another that will be as permanent as possible, marked by the same qualities of commitment, mutuality, giving-and-receiving, union, and tenderness, as will be found in the heterosexual relationship.

7. When a man or a woman "sins," sexually speaking, by actions which deny his faithfulness, mutuality, commitment, tenderness, etc., he may be restored to the path of proper and healthy growth. Ultimately, this forgiveness is from the divine Lover whom we call God; that Lover accepts the "sinner" in the confident hope that through the influence of divine grace (i.e., the empowering possible to those who open themselves to, and ask for, continuing love) something good may be won, in spite of what has been wrong in the past. Proximately, forgiveness is through acceptance in love by other human beings, who surround the "sinner" with their concern and provide opportunities for him to make a fresh start.

8. In sexual life, as everywhere else in man's existence, he is part of society. Hence any decisions he makes, any good that he achieves, any failures that he makes too, affect others and seriously influence the social life. Thus one must ever be mindful of the wide-range consequences of actions for which one decides.

9. In any and every yearning really to love, really to be open to another's love, God is present and God is at work. This tells us that no human being should be *afraid* to love or *fearful* of accepting love. At the same time, since God as Love seeks always the right growth of his human children, their proper movement towards fulfilment, their genuine "making" of personality in social intercourse, this also tells us that we need to be alert to his "guiding." The "guidance" of God is not dictation

88

nor verbal direction; it is found when a man keeps his eyes open, uses his head, and thus sees opportunities for good opening before him. One of those opportunities is given when he meets another with whom he can share life. Yet the sharing of life itself demands that one shall be loyal, controlled, ready to sacrifice for the other—even to sacrifice what may appear attractive possibilities of sexual contact with a third person. And it is right there that love demands more even than control: it demands difficult decisions of a negative sort, precisely in order that the earlier positive decision for the loved one may be maintained.

Chapter 9
God as Love

Throughout this book, stress has been laid upon the specific Christian conviction that love is not only a human affair but is also deepest and highest in the structure of things. The religious man states this conviction when he says that *God is Love* or that *God is Lover*. We have tried to relate human sexual desire and drive to this underlying affirmation. Now, in a closing chapter, it may be useful to turn away from the specifically human (and sexual) application and speak of the "theology of Love"— that is, the implications of the belief that the divine reality whom men worship is "pure unbounded love."

The logical progress in our thought would have been to *begin* rather than end with this chapter. But I have chosen to put it at the end because I believe that it is always better to begin a discussion where people are— and so our opening chapter discussed the problem of sexuality today. We went on to speak of man's nature and the place of his sexuality in that nature. Now that we have done this and have also looked at various aspects of human sexuality, it will be appropriate to indicate clearly and without any attempt at equivocation the underlying religious position of our entire argument.

No theology—and no religion—which fails to put God as Love in the very centre of its thinking can claim to be Christian. In the past, alas, the tendency to put rationality or power or moral righteousness in the central place has led to a distortion of Christian faith. What we need desperately, in my judgement, is to take with utmost seriousness the words which Wesley addressed to God in one of his hymns: "Pure universal Love thou art." This point was brought home most vividly not long ago when at Evensong in my college chapel the anthem was Armstrong Gibbs' beautiful setting of Edmund Spenser's equally beautiful words:

> So let us love, dear love, like as we ought.
> Love is the lesson which the Lord us taught.

As I heard these words, I realized, first, how the whole of Christian life in practice may be summed up in the one term "love," and second, that since love *is* the meaning of the whole Christian enterprise, our failure to make this obvious to the world is more than an omission: it is a denial of what Christianity stands for and means, not only in respect to men but also in respect to God's nature and his way of acting in the world.

How then can one best make an approach to such a theology of love?

Today, certainly, we must begin by talking of the human situation. That is what we have done in this book. The deepest thing in each man is not his rationality, his capacity to think and understand ideas and concepts, important as this is; it is his strong desire; in the words of one of the collects at Eastertide, his "affections"; his yearning to love and to be loved. It is in our loving, in our deepest desiring, that we reveal ourselves most surely for what we are. And it is our desiring which leads us to exert ourselves in what we call our will.

The great Danish writer of the last century, Sören Kierkegaard, once remarked that the meaning of the phrase "purity of heart" is "to will *one thing*" and to will it intensely. Of course he was right, but behind the willing is the desiring. True "purity of heart" is to love that which is truly lovable, most real, most abiding, genuinely excellent; *then* the willing of that good becomes possible for us.

Now what this means for Christians is that man, who is being created by God as he decides in this and that way towards the fulfilment of his possibilities, is made *for* love, precisely because he has been made *in* love and *by* love. This is man's true nature, in the divine intention or purpose. Our human problem, unfortunately, as each man knows for himself when he looks deeply into his own nature, is that we have "unruly wills" because we have "unruly affections." We come to love, hence desire, the second-best, or the third; we tend towards the easily available, the cheap, the shoddy, because they are obviously "at hand." By deciding for these, we compound and increase the misery and pain in the world. Yet deep underneath, there is the call to love and the yearning to be loved—these cannot be eradicated. They are the "image of God" in man.

Our greatest need is for the release of our energies so that we shall learn to love aright, move in the right direction, care for that which is worthy of such devotion. This is what God "commands" of us: not that we shall destroy or deny ourselves, but that we shall desire and seek for the true good which alone can give us enduring joy. And that means movement towards fulfilment. The right pattern and the right priorities in our loving are our deepest need.

It is at this point that the gospel which the church proclaims can become relevant. For underneath all the words which Christians use is the deep conviction that the truly abiding love is to be spelled with an upper-case "L": it is Love, God as Love, God the Lover, in whom Christian faith rightly understood puts its whole trust and confidence. Nor is this taken to be a matter of speculation or theorizing. On the contrary, it is based upon historical events and their significance as men have responded to them. The centre in history for the Christian conviction is Jesus Christ, in whom we have the place and point where the mystery of existence becomes the meaning of human life—which is another way of phrasing what the theologians call "the Incarnation of God in Jesus Christ." Together, that mystery and that meaning spell "Love in action."

This is not sentimentality, as some think; it is not advocacy of a policy of *laissez-faire* in life; it is not easy-going toleration of whatever comes along. It is in fact Love in its most profound sense, Love-in-act, which is searching, demanding, and at the same time alluring and compelling. This Love-in-act is brought vividly and decisively to a focus in Jesus and the response made to him. It is seen in his dealings with others, his giving of himself for others to the point of death, his ability to share with others the victory of Love over hatred—and with it, of good over evil and of life over death. The mystery and the meaning is the Love which is not only *like* the love thus disclosed actively in the total fact of Jesus Christ; it *is* that love seen as the reflection in time and space and human personality of the "Love that moves the sun and the other stars," in Dante's great phrase.

God, then, is the Love that is both personalized and personalizing—

that is no *thing* but personal activity; that makes *us* personal too, as we answer it. Man, we have seen, is personality in the making; and his personality is being made whenever and to the degree that he responds to love, first the Love that is God and then the love that reflects the love of God wherever found. God as Love goes out of himself and ceaselessly gives of himself; he is the Love which cares and which shares. He is the Love "which will not let me go." He is the Love that is affected by whatever happens in the world, yet is undefeated and undefeatable because it is inexhaustible and indefatigable. It is *this* which is placarded before men, enacted in their midst, brought to bear upon their lives, in Jesus Christ—and in a degree elsewhere unequalled and nowhere paralleled.

The remarkable thing is that when Love is thus placarded, enacted, and brought to bear upon men, they can respond to it. This capacity to respond, through our returning love, is (as we have said) the divine image in man, in which we are made. We have been created *in* Love and *by* Love; hence we are made *for* love. If man were nothing but a corrupt and hopeless mess, with no such capacity to respond, the significance of his own little loving would be denigrated. But it is *not* the case that man is utterly unable to respond. He can, he does, respond, even if in partial ways, sporadic, inadequate, misdirected so often and so tragically. The trouble with man is that in his response to Love, and to love, he is "unruly": he is "mixed up," in a situation and condition where true loving is so often frustrated and so readily distorted.

The proclamation of the Christian gospel is the assertion, however, that to men and women who are like this—and that means all of us—the enormously persuasive reality of God's love, brought near in Christ, will work towards a change in men. Once that Love is wholeheartedly accepted, it begins to affect men. For most of them, this comes about slowly and gradually; for a few suddenly and catastrophically. Then "salvation" or wholeness of living is on the way to being established in men. Theology speaks of men's being "saved."

But what are they saved *from?* From lovelessness, meanness, cheapness, superficiality, hypocrisy, wrongful self-assertion. What are they saved *to?* To the Love which is God and hence to the loving which they may know one of another. They are on the way to becoming lovers of God, lovers of others, lovers of men seen in God and of God seen in men. That signifies that they are becoming "authentic men," as contemporary existentialist writers like to say: "authentic" because truly themselves, becoming what they were created and intended to be. They are given strength to overcome the wrongly-directed "loving" which would cut off true development as personalities—the thing which more than all else produces the hatred and awfulness in social existence as well as in individual lives and is responsible for the wars and conflicts which afflict both.

If the Christian understanding of God and his way with men follows this line, our entire theology needs to be constructed in the light of it. Very difficult problems must be faced, for evil is real and to hold such a faith in the face of evil is no easy matter. But we shall have the right direction in our thinking; and the problems which are posed will be the *real* issues of faith, not the irrelevant issues which so much of the time seem to engage the theologian. Perhaps we shall be brought to see that we possess, and can possess, no *solutions;* perhaps we shall learn that the *only* answer is discovered as we proceed—that as we engage in the "works of love" we shall prove "on our pulses" (in Keats' phrase) the truth of Crashaw's tremendous affirmation that "Love is sole sovereign Lord."

Furthermore, perhaps we shall learn that moral codes are of value only as they bespeak love and suggest love and ask for love. Their purpose will be seen as very simple indeed: to make love possible. Whatever does not further love will be meaningless or irrelevant or conventional, not vitally Christian.

Only when we learn "the lesson which the Lord us taught"—and taught in act as well as and more than in words—can men have genuine security. Here we must be very careful lest we think of "security" in superficial ways, as if more "things" were all we needed. Obviously human beings need "things" and they must be given them if life is to be a possibility. Nobody can be indifferent to "things." But the security about which we are now talking is not found in "things"; it is found in something beyond "the changes and chances of this mortal life." It rests upon what *we are becoming,* rather than upon what we *have.* For even if all the "things" we needed were provided—and it is part of Christian concern to see that they *are* provided—they could not guarantee a *lasting* good. "Things" are too fleeting and uncertain. True security is based on God's eternal changelessness, which means something very different from static, inert, and motionless abstraction. God's "changelessness" is his unfailing, utterly faithful, inexhaustible, unalterable reality as Love.

Once desires have been set on that—known to us mostly through given occasions of human experience of loving, but crowned in the event of Jesus Christ, which fulfils and corrects the rest—inner peace is possible for men. In such Love, known through our own being loved and learning to love, we are delivered from falsity into truth, from bondage into freedom. This is what the New Testament calls "the glorious liberty of the children of God," which frees them to live rightly and to labour loyally towards making this world a place where *more* love, and hence more of Love, is known in more places, to more people, in more ways.

I believe that all this is related to and is tied in with what has been said about human sexuality. Otherwise I should not have written this book.